A SELF-STUDY COURSE ON POLITICAL ISLAM

LEVEL 1

A THREE LEVEL COURSE

BILL WARNER, EDITOR

A SELF-STUDY COURSE ON POLITICAL ISLAM
LEVEL 1

A THREE LEVEL COURSE

BILL WARNER, EDITOR

ISBN13   978-1-936659-09-8
ALL RIGHTS RESERVED
V 06.13.11

PUBLISHED BY CSPI, LLC
WWW.CSPIPUBLISHING.COM

PRINTED IN THE USA

TABLE OF CONTENTS

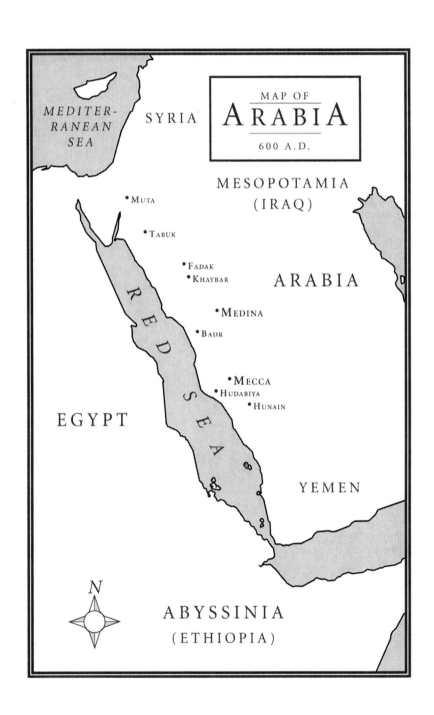

INTRODUCTION

THIS BOOK

Until now studying Islam has always been done by scholars—university scholars and Islamic scholars. The university scholars are from the history, Arabic language, religion and Middle East studies departments. Each of these areas has its own narrow view of Islam. In the past, they've told us that Islam is very complicated and difficult to understand. Why? A university professor wants to be viewed as learned and intelligent. He wants you to think that he is the master of a very difficult and obscure topic. The same thing is true of an imam (a religious leader of Islam).

After September 11, 2001, the attack on the World Trade Center and the Pentagon, Islam started receiving attention of a new kind of scholarship, scholarship that is not based on Arabic, history or religion. This new scholarship uses critical thought and analytic techniques that are based on science.

The scientific method is a new method to study Islam. Critical analysis shows that Islam is both a religion and a political system and that the political system is the greatest part of Islamic doctrine.

THE TRILOGY

Most people think that Islam is based on the Koran. However, there is not enough information to practice the religion of Islam. The Koran says in 91 verses for every Muslim to copy Mohammed in the smallest detail of life. There are two books that give us Mohammed—the Sira (his biography) and the Hadith (small stories and sayings).

The Trilogy is made up of three books—

• The Koran is what Mohammed said that the angel Gabriel said that Allah said. But the Koran does not contain enough guidance for one to be a Muslim, except by repeatedly telling us that all of the world

1

should imitate Mohammed in every way. Mohammed's words and deeds are called the Sunna. The Sunna is found in two different texts—the Sira and Hadith.

- The first source of the Sunna is the Sira which is Mohammed's biography.

- The other source of the Sunna is the Hadith, the Traditions of Mohammed. There are several versions of the Hadith, but the most commonly used is by Bukhari.

So the Trilogy is the Koran, Sira and Hadith. The Koran is the smallest part of Islam's "bible". If we count the words in each text we find that Islam is 16% Allah and 84% Mohammed.

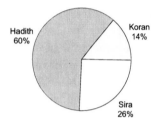

The Relative Sizes of the Trilogy Texts

Hadith 60%
Koran 14%
Sira 26%

All of the foundations of Islamic doctrine are found in the Trilogy. Once you know the Trilogy, you know all of the foundations of Islam.

There is very good news here. If you understand Mohammed's life, you understand the greatest part of Islam. Anybody can understand the biography of a man. Mohammed was born, was raised an orphan, became a businessman, then a prophet. In his last phase of life, he became a politician and warrior. When he died every Arab in his sphere was a Muslim and he did not have an enemy left standing. Anyone can read and understand his life and therefore understand Islam.

KAFIR

The word, Kafir, is usually translated as "unbeliever" but this translation is wrong. The word "unbeliever" is logically and emotionally neutral, whereas Kafir is the most abusive, prejudiced and hateful word in any language. The Koran says that the Kafir may be deceived, plotted against, hated, enslaved, mocked, tortured and worse.

There are many religious names for Kafirs: polytheists, idolaters, People of the Book (Christians and Jews), Buddhists, atheists, agnostics, and pagans. Kafir covers them all, because no matter what the religious name is, they can all be treated in the same way. What Mohammed said and did to polytheists can be done to any other category of Kafir.

Islam devotes a great amount of energy to the Kafir. The majority (64%) of the Koran is devoted to the Kafir, and nearly all of the Sira (81%) deals with Mohammed's struggle with them. The Hadith (Traditions) devotes

2

32% of the text to Kafirs[1]. Overall, the Trilogy devotes 60% of its content to the Kafir.

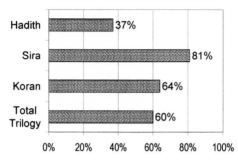

Amount of Text Devoted to the Kafir

Here are a few of the Koran references:

A Kafir can be mocked—

Koran83:34 *On that day the faithful will mock the Kafirs, while they sit on bridal couches and watch them. Should not the Kafirs be paid back for what they did?*

A Kafir can be beheaded—

Koran47:4 *When you encounter the Kafirs on the battlefield, cut off their heads until you have thoroughly defeated them and then take the prisoners and tie them up firmly.*

A Kafir can be plotted against—

Koran86:15 *They plot and scheme against you [Mohammed], and I plot and scheme against them. Therefore, deal calmly with the Kafirs and leave them alone for a while.*

A Kafir can be terrorized—

Koran8:12 *Then your Lord spoke to His angels and said, "I will be with you. Give strength to the believers. I will send terror into the Kafirs' hearts, cut off their heads and even the tips of their fingers!"*

A Muslim is not the friend of a Kafir—

Koran3:28 *Believers should not take Kafirs as friends in preference to other believers. Those who do this will have none of Allah's protection and will only have themselves as guards. Allah warns you to fear Him for all will return to Him.*

---

1   http://cspipublishing.com/statistical/TrilogyStats/AmtTxtDevoted-Kafir.html

A Kafir is evil—

> Koran23:97 *And say: Oh my Lord! I seek refuge with You from the suggestions of the evil ones [Kafirs]. And I seek refuge with you, my Lord, from their presence.*

A Kafir is disgraced—

> Koran37:18 *Tell them, "Yes! And you [Kafirs] will be disgraced."*

A Kafir is cursed—

> Koran33:60 *They [Kafirs] will be cursed, and wherever they are found, they will be seized and murdered. It was Allah's same practice with those who came before them, and you will find no change in Allah's ways.*

KAFIRS AND PEOPLE OF THE BOOK

Muslims tell Christians and Jews that they are special. They are "People of the Book" and are brothers in the Abrahamic faith. But in Islam you are a Christian, if and only if, you believe that Christ was a man who was a prophet of Allah; there is no Trinity; Jesus was not crucified nor resurrected and that He will return to establish Sharia law. To be a true Jew you must believe that Mohammed is the last in the line of Jewish prophets.

This verse is positive:

> Koran5:77 *Say: Oh, People of the Book, do not step out of the bounds of truth in your religion, and do not follow the desires of those who have gone wrong and led many astray. They have themselves gone astray from the even way.*

Islamic doctrine is dualistic, so there is an opposite view as well. Here is the last verse written about the People of the Book (A later verse abrogates or nullifies an earlier verse. See page 26.). This is the final word. It calls for Muslims to make war on the People of the Book who do not believe in the religion of truth, Islam.

> Koran9:29 *Make war on those who have received the Scriptures [Jews and Christians] but do not believe in Allah or in the Last Day. They do not forbid what Allah and His Messenger have forbidden. The Christians and Jews do not follow the religion of truth until they submit and pay the poll tax [jizya] and they are humiliated.*

The sentence "They do not forbid..." means that they do not accept Sharia law; "until they submit" means to submit to Sharia law. Christians and Jews who do not accept Mohammed as the final prophet are Kafirs.

Muslims pray five times a day and the opening prayer always includes:

Koran1: 7 *Not the path of those who anger You [the Jews] nor the path of those who go astray [the Christians].*

LANGUAGE

Since the original Arabic word for unbelievers was Kafir and that is the actual word used in the Koran and Sharia law, that is the word used here for accuracy and precision.

It is very simple: if you don't believe Mohammed was the prophet of Allah, you are a Kafir.

POLITICAL ISLAM

What is the difference between religious Islam and Political Islam? Do you remember when some Danish artists drew some cartoons of Mohammed? There were weeks of rioting, threats, lawsuits, killings, assassinations and destruction by Muslims. If Muslims want to respect Mohammed by never criticizing, joking about him and taking every word he said as a sacred example—that is religious. But when they threaten, pressure and hurt Kafirs for not respecting Mohammed, that is political. When Muslims say that Mohammed is the prophet of the only god, that is religious, but when they insist that Kafirs never disrespect Mohammed, that is political. When the newspapers and TV agreed not to publish the cartoons, that was a political response, not a religious response.

Let's consider the Trilogy. Detailed statistical analysis shows that about sixty percent of the Koran is political in nature. That is, it tells how to relate to Kafirs, not how a Muslim leads a good life. Less than forty percent of the Koran is actually devoted to the religion of Islam. This is a major insight, because when you study Mohammed's life, you also learn that the bulk of it was political, not religious.

Political Islam is the doctrine that relates to the Kafir. Islam's relationship to the Kafir cannot be religious since a Muslim is strictly forbidden to have any religious interaction with them. The religion of Islam is what is required for a Muslim to avoid Hell and enter Paradise.

The Trilogy not only advocates a religious superiority over the Kafir—the Kafirs go to Hell whereas Muslims go to Paradise—but also its doctrine demands that Muslims dominate the Kafir in all politics and culture. This domination is political, not religious.

Islam's success comes primarily from its politics. In thirteen years as a spiritual leader, Mohammed converted 150 people to his religion. When

5

he became a political leader and warrior, Islam exploded in growth, and Mohammed became king of Arabia in ten years.

The power of this course is that you will be able to sort out the religion of Islam from the politics of Islam. As a political system, Islam can be criticized as easily as you can criticize Communism, Nazism, Democrats or Republicans. They are all just political systems. It is still socially acceptable to reject a political system.

THE THREE VIEWS OF ISLAM

There are three points of view relative to Islam. The point of view depends upon how you feel about Mohammed. If you believe Mohammed is the prophet of Allah, then you are a believer. If you don't, you are a Kafir. The third viewpoint is that of an apologist for Islam. Apologists do not believe that Mohammed was a prophet, but they are tolerant about Islam without any actual knowledge of Islam.

Here is an example of the three points of view.

In Medina, Mohammed sat all day long beside his 12-year-old wife while they watched as the heads of 800 Jews were removed by sword.[2] Their heads were cut off because they had said that Mohammed was not the prophet of Allah. Muslims view these deaths as necessary because denying Mohammed's prophet-hood was, and remains, an offense against Islam. They were beheaded because it is sanctioned by Allah.

Kafirs look at this event as proof of the jihadic violence of Islam and as an evil act.

Apologists say that this was an historic event; that all cultures have violence in their past, and no judgment should be passed. They have never actually read any of Islam's foundational texts, but speak authoritatively about Islam.

According to the different points of view, killing the 800 Jews was:

- A perfect sacred act
- A tragedy
- Another historical event. We have done worse.

There is no "right" view of Islam, since the views cannot be reconciled.

This book is written from the Kafir point of view. Everything in this book views Islam from the perspective of how Islam affects Kafirs. This

---

2   *The Life of Muhammad*, A. Guillaume, Oxford University Press, 1982, pg. 464.

also means that the religion is of little importance. A Muslim cares about the religion of Islam, but all Kafirs are affected by Islam's political views.

This book discusses Islam as a political system. It does not discuss Muslims or their religion. Muslims are people and vary from one to another. Religion is what one does to go to Paradise and avoid Hell. It is not useful nor necessary to discuss Islam as a religion.

We must talk about Islam in the political realm, because it is a powerful and ambitious political system.

MUSLIMS

There is one issue that people have when they hear about Islam. At work or school they have met Muslims and they are nice people. So when you hear something grim about Islam, you may think, well, Ahmed is not like that. If Ahmed is so nice, how can these dreadful things be true?

First, this entire course is about Islam, not Muslims. Muslims are people; Islam is a doctrine and an ideology. Before you can understand how Ahmed can be so nice, you must first understand the entirety of Islam. Islam is a dualistic ideology; it always has two answers. This is because there are two Korans and two Mohammeds. When you understand the dual nature of Islam, you will understand how some people, who call themselves Muslims, can be very nice. But you will also understand how they have some moral choices they can make that are not available to you.

This is a fact-based study. You can read the actual doctrine for yourself and draw your own conclusions. You also will never have to ask a Muslim anything about Islam. You will become your own expert. Islam is a most fascinating subject, particularly Political Islam.

REFERENCE NUMBERS

The information in this book can be traced back to the source by use of the following reference numbers:

Koran12:45 is Koran chapter (sura) 12, verse 45.

SPELLING

We have studied Islam so little that there is no standardized spelling of proper Arabic nouns in the English language. Examples: Mohammed/ Muhammad, Muslim/Moslem.

GLOSSARY

There is a glossary of Islamic words at the end of this volume.

MOHAMMED

INTRODUCTION

When you think of a political leader you may think of Napoleon, Alexander the Great or Caesar. They were great generals, but they don't hold a candle to Mohammed, because no one today kills for Napoleon, no one today kills for Caesar, but today it is undoubtedly true that somewhere in the world people are being destroyed because of the perfect example of Mohammed.

If you know Mohammed, then you know Islam. If you do not know Mohammed, you do not know Islam. Every Muslim's life goal is to imitate Mohammed in every detail. Mohammed led a fascinating life—he was a businessman, prophet, politician and warrior. His greatest invention was a political system that can make all others submit.

We're going to study Mohammed before we study the basics of Islam. This is because Mohammed is the origin of Islam and he comes before everything. There was no Islam before Mohammed and he called himself the last of the prophets. In a sense, Islam both begins with Mohammed and ends with Mohammed. The importance of studying Mohammed is found in the Koran itself. The Koran says 91 times that every human being is supposed conduct their life after Mohammed's example. Mohammed is the perfect pattern of life for all peoples for all time.

We know an enormous amount about Mohammed. His biography, the Sira[1], is over 800 pages long and it is in fine print. Then, as if that were not enough, we have what are called the Traditions of Mohammed—also called the Hadith. We have thousands upon thousands of these traditions. We know a lot about this man.

---

1   *The Life of Muhammad*, A. Guillaume (a translation of Ishaq's *Sirat Rasul Allah*), Oxford University Press, Pakistan, 1982.

THE IMPORTANCE OF MOHAMMED

The importance of Mohammed can be found in the religion of Islam. Most Kafirs think that you become a Muslim by worshiping the God Allah, but this is not true. You can worship the God Allah and still not be a Muslim. What it takes to be a Muslim is to worship Allah exactly like Mohammed did, and we know exactly how he worshiped his God. The further importance of Mohammed can be found in this: there is not enough in the Koran to enable you to practice the religion of Islam. For instance, the Koran says to pray, but does not tell how to do Islamic prayer. That information comes from the Hadith. All of the details of how to be a Muslim are found in Mohammed's example, not from the Koran.

There are Five Pillars of Islam which we will study in the next lesson, but there is not enough information in the Koran to practice even one of the Five Pillars. You cannot worship in an Islamic way without imitating Mohammed. Mohammed's way of doing things is so important that it has a very special name: the Sunna, which means the Way.

It is in Mohammed that we find right and wrong, except right and wrong as we think of it in a moral sense is not used within Islam. Instead the concept is: "What is permitted" and "What is forbidden." What is permitted is what Mohammed did. What is forbidden is what he said not to do, or he himself didn't do, so the Sunna of Mohammed is what dictates Islam. To know Islam we have to study Mohammed.

One of the ways that you can tell how much someone knows about Islam is if they mention Mohammed or not. Sometimes you run into people who want to explain Islam on the basis of the Koran. When this happens, you can be sure you have run into a person who does not really understand Islam or is a deceiver. The Koran is not remotely enough to explain Islam, since it is incomplete.

Let's take a very small item. Have you ever been watching a news broadcast and there's some Islamic leader from the Middle East and he's talking and he's angry, perhaps he's shouting. Why do they do this? One simple reason: Mohammed was easily angered. This is recorded in both the Sira and the Hadith, so when you see a Muslim who is quick to anger, he is simply imitating Mohammed.

Mohammed was the perfect father, the perfect husband, religious leader, military leader, and political leader. There is no aspect of life, including business, where a Muslim does not turn to the example of Mohammed. He is the perfect Muslim. There is not a Muslim alive who does not know the life of Mohammed. What is odd is that there are so few Kafirs who know anything about the life of Mohammed. When you study Mohammed it is rather confusing, because he seems to be two very different people.

THE LIFE OF MOHAMMED

Let's quickly review his life. He was an orphan as a child, and later became a businessman. He went on caravan trading trips to Syria. He was prosperous and well thought of in his community. He was seen as a person who could settle arguments and heal disputes. He was a very religious man, and then, in his 40s, he began to go on religious retreats, leaving the city of Mecca and praying by himself. Then he started to hear a voice, and he saw a vision. Now, this was a voice that no one else ever heard, and a vision that no one else ever saw, but it was very important to Mohammed and it completely changed his life and, indeed, his entire character.

After seeing this vision and hearing the voice, he went back to Mecca and began to tell people—first his friends and family—that he had been chosen as the messenger of the only God of the Universe. Later this God was named Allah. Mohammed began to introduce two principles that were to change him and to change the entire world forever.

The first of these principles was submission. Mohammed said that the God of the universe told him to tell everyone else that they were to do exactly what he said when he said it. That their lives were to be patterned after him, that he was the perfect man, the perfect pattern. This created dissension within Mecca because amongst the other things he told the Meccans was that their ancestors were burning in Hell. He then created, at the same time, a second principle called duality. He created a great division between those who believed what he said and those who did not. This was the great division of the Koran—humanity was divided into the believer and nonbeliever, the Muslim and the Kafir.

Mohammed was very aggressive in pushing his message. So much so that he irritated the Meccans. He was not very successful as a consequence, and over the next 13 years, in spite of his daily preaching, he failed to gain many followers. He was argumentative and caused trouble, but the Meccans couldn't do anything about him because he was protected by his uncle who had some power within Mecca. Then, his protector died, and the Meccans told Mohammed, "You'll have to leave. We're sick and tired of living with you. You've created dissension and distress and suffering within our community." So Mohammed went north 100 miles to a town called Medina.

MOHAMMED IN MEDINA

Mohammed became a politician and a warrior and everything changed. He did not succeed by numbers when he was a preacher, but now he became overwhelmingly successful because he created a new concept, the concept of jihad. Jihad totally changed Mohammed and totally changed Islam. Now, through jihad, Islam had a way to get money and lots of it. It had a way to bring about political power.

Here we have the second element of duality that Mohammed introduced. There are two Mohammeds. There is the religious preacher Mohammed, and there is the warrior-politician Mohammed. Duality is one of the things that is confusing about Islam. It always has two messages to preach and the reason it has two messages to preach is that there are two Mohammeds. More than that, when you read the Koran it's clear there are two Korans. One Koran is religious, the other Koran is political; both are combined in the Koran you buy at the bookstore. Mohammed the religious man was not much of a success at all, but Mohammed the political man, and the warrior, was overwhelmingly successful. In the last nine years of his life he averaged an event of violence every six weeks. By this process of constant warfare he became the first ruler of all of Arabia.

Mohammed did not get along well with his neighbors. Even in his religious phase, he was pushy and aggressive. The Meccans didn't like him, they said, "You've created more suffering in this community than we've ever had before." Before he became a Muslim, Mohammed was a good neighbor. After he became the messenger of Allah, he became an aggressive neighbor. When he went to Medina, his behavior became even worse.

As an example—when he moved to Medina, half the town was Jewish. Within three years after he arrived, all the Jews had been either driven out of Medina—after their money was taken—or they'd been killed and sold into slavery. But after Mohammed had conquered all of Medina, being a hostile neighbor had a new meaning. If you lived even 100 miles away, Mohammed would show up with his arms and troops and demand that you submit to Allah. Once he ruled all of Arabia, he was still a hostile neighbor. Before Mohammed died, he had struck out to the north to Syria to fight the Christians. His dying words were: "Let there be neither Jew nor Christian left in Arabia."

Mohammed was the most successful military man who ever lived. As political leader he became all-powerful. We have other examples in history of men who became all-powerful and we can measure to some degree how powerful they were by how many people died because of them. The person who in our known history killed the most people was Mao Tse-Tung.

As far as we can tell, figures show that through starvation and persecution and outright executions, Mao Tse-Tung was responsible for the deaths of 40 million people[1].

Now we come to Mohammed. Mohammed has influenced the deaths—through his principle of jihad and aggressive politics—of 270 million people. Now this has taken over 1400 years. Mao killed 40 million within his lifetime. But still, the total of those that Mao killed is fewer than those who were killed in imitation of Mohammed.

THE PERSON

Mohammed had a very dualistic personality. He had a sense of humor, he loved children. He wept when his favorite warrior was killed. But at the same time he was a soft-spoken man who laughed heartily when the head of one of his enemies was thrown at his feet. He was the perfect slaveholder and slave trader. Indeed, one of the ways he financed jihad was through the sale of slaves. He got his slaves in the time-honored way of killing their protectors. He attacked a tribe, killed the male members until the rest surrendered and then they were given a choice to convert. If they didn't, they were sold into slavery. Women, children, men. This was profitable and, indeed, jihad was profitable. He used jihad to finance more jihad. Mohammed came up with a way to make religion and politics pay and pay well.

Mohammed was a very intolerant man. This is interesting. Before Mohammed, Arabs were noted for their religious tolerance. Indeed, Mecca, the town where Mohammed first rose to power, had over 360 religions. No man was ever injured because of his religion until Mohammed. Mohammed converted the Arab from being a tolerant person to the most intolerant person and the reason that the Arab became intolerant was they followed the Sunna of Mohammed.

One of the conventions regarding Mohammed today is that no one can tell a joke about him without dire results. You hear jokes about Jesus, Noah, Adam, St. Peter, God, but you never hear a Mohammed joke. You may remember when a Danish cartoonist said "Let's have a contest and see who can draw the best Mohammed cartoon." People died because of those cartoons because Islam was offended. You can't make a joke about Mohammed, not even one. In fact, in Pakistan and other Muslim countries, to tell a joke about Mohammed is literally a death sentence.

---

1   http://necrometrics.com/20c5m.htm

There's one more thing about Mohammed which explains Muslims and Islam. He never forgot a slight or an insult. Never. When he re-entered Mecca—this time triumphant after the jihad in Medina—the first thing he did, and here we have the essence of the man Mohammed, the first thing he did was to pray, the second thing he did was to have all religious art destroyed. So the religious objects of 360 religions in Mecca were destroyed. Mohammed helped to build the fire and break the objects. The next thing he did was to issue death warrants for five different people who'd criticized him. These were intellectuals, not warriors. For instance, two of the people who were killed were dancing girls. What had they done? They had been in a skit, with a song and a poem that ridiculed Mohammed. Mohammed never forgot a insult. Similarly, Islamic memory is long for any suffering.

Mohammed is the most common name in the world even after 1400 years. He continues to be the most influential politician and warrior who ever lived. His life as the Messenger of Allah shapes the ethics, morals, politics and culture of over a billion Muslims. His politics have annihilated half of ancient Christianity, Hinduism and Buddhism.

THE BASICS

Almost everyone thinks of Islam as a religion but as you're going to discover, religion is the least of Islam. Islam is an entire civilization. It's a culture, a legal system, a thought system, and an ethical system. Islam is all encompassing.

The most important fact about Islam is that it is a political ideology. The religion is of secondary importance. The religion is based upon the Five Pillars. The politics are based upon jihad, the sixth pillar. Islam divides all of the world into believers and Kafirs. When you understand the concept of Kafir, you will understand all of Political Islam.

THE FIVE PILLARS

The religion of Islam is simple. It's based upon the Five Pillars. The first of these pillars is there is no God but Allah and Mohammed is his prophet. If you say that in Arabic in front of other Muslims you have become a Muslim. It is the most central aspect of Islam, acknowledging both the Koran and the Sunna (Mohammed's perfect example). Allah is not enough to be a Muslim, you must have the perfect example of Mohammed.

The next pillar is charity. The *zakat* is a charity tax but it is quite different from what most of us think of as charity. First of all, Muslim charity goes to Muslims; it does *not* go to Kafirs.

There's another difference: money given to an Islamic charity can support jihad. It can support the creation of jihad and it is also specifically for helping those whose family members have died in jihad.

Another of the five pillars is prayer. Muslims are famous for their attitude towards prayer which is done five times a day and even in public places. After prayer we have the Haj, the pilgrimage to Mecca. This is supposed to be done once in every Muslim's life if he can afford it.

Another religious obligation is to fast every year in the month of Ramadan. Now fasting for a Muslim means that you don't eat or drink when the sun is up. At night you can eat and drink as much as you wish.

JIHAD

Those are the religious five pillars. Then there is a sixth pillar. The sixth pillar is jihad. The reason jihad is called a pillar of Islam is that just like the other five it is incumbent upon all Muslims without exception. All Muslims are supposed to participate in jihad. We will have an entire lesson on jihad later, but just because a Muslim is supposed to participate in jihad does not mean that he's actually involved in the jihad of the sword. Jihad can be done with the sword, with the mouth, with a pen and with money, but more about that later.

Jihad is both religious and political. Islam is primarily a political doctrine, not a religious doctrine. For instance, the Koran is more concerned with the Kafir, than it is the believer. It spends 64% of its time discussing the Kafir; only 36% of the Koran is about Islam and the Muslim[1]. The Koran spends so much time talking about the Kafir that we must address that issue now.

KAFIR

A Muslim is forbidden to enter into any religious aspect of life with a Kafir. That is, Islam treats the Kafir as being outside of Islam and has an extensive doctrine on how to deal with Kafirs.

As an example of the political nature of being a Kafir, there are many, many references in the Koran to Hell and the Kafir is in Hell, but the reason a Kafir is in Hell is not because he did anything that was morally wrong such as theft or murder, but simply because the Kafir did not believe that Mohammed was the prophet of Allah. So Islamic Hell is a political prison for intellectual dissenters.

The other basic thing about Islam is that it does not have the Golden Rule. Indeed Islam denies the truth of the Golden Rule. In Islam there is no such thing as humanity. Instead the world is always seen as being divided into the Kafir and the believer. Humanity is not seen as one body.

Once you have that fundamental division, you no longer have the Golden Rule because the Golden Rule is to treat others as you would want to be treated and that means all others. Islam does not work like that. Islam instead is based upon submission and duality. Submission because the word Islam means submission and that all others must submit to Islam. Now all others having to submit to Islam is also a political statement.

---

1 http://cspipublishing.com/statistical/TrilogyStats/AmtTxtDevotedKafir.html

The political aspect of submission is that the Kafir must submit to the Muslim and Islam.

The other principle that Islam is based upon is duality. We will see this in great detail when we study the Koran, but we've already seen duality in the Mohammed of Mecca and the Mohammed of Medina and those two men were not the same.

POLITICAL ISLAM

Islam is the most successful political system on the face of the earth. For 1400 years Islam has slowly expanded. In only two cases in the history of Islam has it ever been driven back. One in Spain in 1492 and the other in Eastern Europe in 1683. Other than those two times Islam keeps expanding. It expands on a daily basis. Indeed as we will discover later, the power of Political Islam increases every day in Europe and the United States.

We like to think that liberal democracy is the most powerful force on the face of the earth, but liberal democracy is only 200 years old, and is very difficult to implement, whereas Political Islam is 1400 years old and is quite easy to implement. And once it is in place, it always stays in place. Once a nation becomes Islamic the only thing that can change it is force from the outside as occurred in Spain, where the Moors were driven out of Spain. Otherwise there has never been a case of a revolution inside of an Islamic country. By revolution here we mean one that eliminated Islam as the driving political force, not a change of rulers.

Political Islam is very effective. There have been over 270 million people killed by jihad over the last 1400 years. Islam has also been very successful in the business of slavery. For 1400 years it has enslaved the Kafir and we will have an entire lesson on how Islam has enslaved the European, the African and the Asian. Political Islam is a phenomenally successful political ideology.

NOT MUSLIMS

Twenty percent of the world is Islamic. The other 80% is made up of Kafirs. We need to understand that Kafir culture includes the Christian, the Jew, the Hindu, the atheist and the Buddhist. It includes Chinese, Australians, and Africans. It includes the animist, that is those who believe that the world is a spirit affair. So Kafirs are everybody but Muslims. Now here's what's important about that. Kafirs need to understand that so far as Islam is concerned, there is not the slightest bit of difference how a Kafir is treated whether he's an atheist, a Christian, a Jew, or a Hindu. It doesn't make any difference. For instance, Christians make a great deal of distinctions amongst themselves and for that matter so do Buddhists, but from the viewpoint of Islam, all Kafirs are the same. They deny Mohammed. They deny the Sunna of Mohammed, that is the way of Mohammed, and all Kafirs deny the truth of the Koran. Kafirs are all those who don't believe that Mohammed is the Prophet of Allah.

An infidel can only be a Jew or a Christian; therefore the term infidel is a religious term. Another term used by Islam is polytheist, many gods. This, too, is a religious term. Atheist is a religious term. And one last term that Islam uses for the Kafir is Peoples of the Book and this refers again to Christians and Jews. Those terms, pagan, infidel, polytheist, atheist and People of the Book are religious words. And remember this lesson series is not at all about the religion. That's the reason Kafir is the word to use because an infidel is a Kafir. A polytheist is a Kafir, a pagan is a Kafir, an atheist is a Kafir and the People of the Book are Kafirs as well. So we will use the term Kafir.

We will be studying the deaths of 270 million Kafirs over 1400 years in jihad. That's 60 million Christians, 80 million Hindus, 10 million Buddhists and 120 million Africans of varying religions[1]. But now we have to recognize one more thing about the Kafir, and that is this: Kafirs display little interest in learning about Islam. We will study in this series why Kafirs never refer to the injury of Islam, why Kafir Christians don't know how Turkey and Egypt went from being Christian to Islamic. Why do Buddhists never talk about the fact that Islam has killed 10 million Buddhists? You can find some Hindus who are willing to discuss the destruction of 80 million Hindus but they're rare. So one of the things that we will study in this series is why Kafirs fear and dread Islam so much that Kafirs refuse to study their own history. We will study why European Kafirs never refer to the fact that a million Europeans were taken into slavery. Kafirs and Islam is what this entire series is about. It's all about the politics of Islam.

Since Islam is a complete civilization, that is to say, since Islam contains everything that it needs within itself, it has no need of the Kafir civilization. It annihilates the Kafir's civilization. In every case, once Islam rises to political power in a country, the original civilization is annihilated. When you go to Egypt today you do not see any sign of the original Coptic or Christian civilization that was in Egypt. It is gone. Everything about it has disappeared. Even the names that people use, the names for cities, all change. Islam is a complete civilization and therefore when a country

---

1 *Mohammed and the Unbelievers*, Bill Warner, CSPI Publishing, 2010, pg. 160.

becomes fully Islamicized there is no trace whatsoever of the original civilization and that is one of the marks of Islamic politics.

The basics of Islam are the Five Pillars, jihad, submission, duality and the Kafir. Once you understand those words, you can understand how Political Islam has annihilated civilizations for 1400 years.

JIHAD

Jihad was Mohammed's greatest invention. It made him successful. Jihad is a misunderstood word. Most jihad is done with money and persuasion, not violence. It is jihad that fills Washington DC with money to buy influence. It is jihad that causes our textbooks in our schools to never mention anything negative about Islam.

Jihad is surely one of the more famous Arabic words. Jihad does not mean holy war, although it includes holy war. Jihad actually means struggle, which is a much better way to see it because jihad includes much more than war with violence. Jihad can be done with the sword, the mouth, the pen and with money. The Koran defines jihad as fighting in Allah's cause.

Amount of Trilogy Text Devoted to Jihad

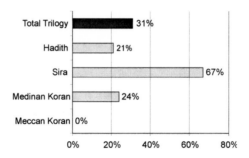

The Koran lays out the vision of jihad. The Sira (Mohammed's biography) lays out the grand strategy of jihad. The hadith (the Traditions) give us the tactics—all the small details about what needs to be done. And of course all of these things are modeled upon Mohammed, because Mohammed is not only the perfect Muslim, but also the perfect jihadist. You can see how important jihad is when you read Mohammed's biography. Jihad takes up about two-thirds of the Sira. There was only a nine-year period in which he pursued intense jihad but the number of pages that are devoted to it gives you an idea of how important it was. The importance is this: Mohammed did not succeed until he turned to jihad. It's only natural that Muslims would look to jihad as their most successful strategy and therefore record the most about it.

THE REAL JIHAD

Now let's take care of one issue. Muslims frequently say, ' Well, the real jihad is inner struggle, the spiritual struggle." That is the Greater Jihad. The jihad of the sword and war is the Lesser Jihad. But the hadith tell us about the greater jihad—the inner spiritual struggle. But only 2%[1] of the hadith are devoted to this kind of struggle. The other 98% are about killing the Kafir. Is jihad the inner struggle? Yes. Is jihad killing the Kafir? Yes. Notice again we have a duality. There are two ways to view jihad. A Muslim may choose whichever he need for the moment. Let's look at an example that everyone remembers. On September 11, 2001 the World Trade Center and the Pentagon were attacked by Muslims in an act of jihad. It was said by Muslims that that the jihadists had hijacked their religion. But let's look and see, because when you understand jihad as it comes from the Koran, the Sira, and the Hadith you will discover that everything about 9/11 was by the book.

This was not the first time the World Trade Center had been attacked by jihadists. In 1993, an attempt was made to bring down the Twin Towers with a massive bomb placed in the basement. That didn't work, but it didn't matter because the second time it did. The second time was practiced over and over. When it all came down on September 11 they had been through it many times. This is modeled on the example of Mohammed.

When Mohammed turned to jihad, the first time he sent his men out to kill and rob, they failed. They didn't find anyone to rob. The second try was also a failure, as was the third and several subsequent attempts. But when they went out for the eighth time, they were successful. 9/11 is just like Mohammed's jihad.

Another way it was like jihad was that Muslims after 9/11 said "we're the real victims. Muslims were the ones who were really hurt." Again, this is precisely like Mohammed did it. When his eighth attack was successful he was accused by the Arabs of violating all the rules of war because he attacked during the holy month of Ramadan. The Koran replied to this and said that what the Meccans—the Kafirs—had done to Mohammed was far more serious than being killed. It was true that the Meccan Arabs had run Mohammed out of the city, but they didn't harm anyone. When

---

1   http://cspipublishing.com/statistical/TrilogyStats/Greater-jihad.html

the Muslims killed the Kafirs they said, "We're the real victims here, not the dead Kafirs."

Another way in which 9/11 was modeled after Mohammed is this: Muslims claimed "Oh, we are the religion of peace." The veil of the religion of Islam was used to hide the political act of jihad. This has been done before as well. Mohammed always covered his political actions with a religious necessity.

The World Trade Center was chosen as a target for two reasons. The first reason is it was a trade center, a business center. It was the hope of Al Qaeda and Osama bin Laden that destroying the World Trade Center would paralyze the American economy. Because you see, jihad wherever possible is an economic attack. Mohammed's attacks on the caravans were to gain wealth for himself and to remove wealth from the Kafirs.

CLASSICAL JIHAD AND 9/11

When he attacked towns he destroyed the farms outside the town. Like 9/11 this was a form of economic warfare. Now the second reason that the World Trade Center was attacked was that Zawaheri, seemingly the key planner, was told that there were a lot of Jews there. This again was just like Mohammed because Mohammed persecuted Jews of Medina and Khaybar and Ladak.

Another way that 9/11 was modeled after Mohammed's actions is this. The men who did it were immigrants to this country. Mohammed did not take up jihad until he was an emigrant. When he moved to Medina he called that his "immigration." How important is this immigration? Well, "Islamic Time" starts when he entered Medina and became a politician and warrior. That's the reason why all Islamic calendars start with that time and not with the time of Mohammed's first revelation, which might seem to be the Time Zero for Islam. Time Zero was chosen because of immigration, the beginning of Mohammed's political success.

As a sneak attack, 9/11 also followed Mohammed's method. He used sneak attacks whenever possible. So on 9/11 when we woke up to terror and fire, it was just as though Mohammed had ordered it.

The attack on the World Trade Center violated the rules of war, another of Mohammed's tactics. One of the reasons that Mohammed always beat the Arabs was because they kept expecting him to play by the rules. After all, before Mohammed there were established rules of war. But when Mohammed developed jihad he threw out all the rules. Brother would kill brother, father would kill son, tribe member would go to war against another tribe member. This violated all the rules of Arabian war, but Mohammed knew how to win, and that was to violate the rules.

Another way that September 11 was very Mohammedan was there was no shame or remorse inside of the Islamic community. The most popular book in the Arab world after 9/11 was written by a man who had shared a jail cell with Zawaheri. And his criticism of Zawaheri was not that what they had done was immoral. No. What was wrong was it woke the sleeping tiger, America. Many Muslims expressed no remorse over 3000 dead Kafirs because at no time in Mohammed's life did he ever express the slightest remorse over the death of a Kafir. Indeed we have records in which he laughed and cheered, when Kafirs suffered[1].

Here's an interesting thing about the attack on the World Trade Center. Two days after it happened, telephones begin to ring in churches all across America and when the church member picked up the phone, the other person said "I'm a Muslim and we would like to come to your church and give a seminar on Islam, the peaceful religion."

Now, this was a great deception, but it was also done with amazing speed and power. Think about it. Do you know of any other group, Democrat, Republican, military—anything in the world—that could with, only 48 hours notice, launch a uniform public relations attack across an entire nation?

Another clue that 9/11 was modeled after Mohammed is that we were called to Islam before the attack. That was Mohammed's way also. Osama bin Laden issued a videotape in which he condemned America and then called America to Islam. If America had come to Islam —I guess in this case, if George Bush had decided to become a Muslim—there would not have been an attack. The call to Islam was issued first. This was patterned after Mohammed's perfect jihad.

September 11 was a defensive attack. All jihad is defensive because the Kafir creates the first offense by denying Mohammed. So the Kafir has already offended Allah. Therefore, what follows the offense is a defensive attack. If it were not for the Kafir there would be no jihad.

And this brings us to something else that we need to know. According to Islamic doctrine jihad is eternal and is incumbent upon all Muslims. Jihad is not to cease until the last Kafir has submitted. As long as there are Kafirs there will be jihad.

Soon after 9/11 Islam started attacking the Kafirs by calling them Crusaders. Now the Crusades are portrayed as evil by Islam. But why did the

---

1   *The Life of Muhammad*, A. Guillaume, Oxford University Press, Karachi, 1982, pg. 675

Crusaders go to an Arabian, Muslim Middle East? They went to help the Christians who cried out for help. That's how it all started. It wasn't a band of Europeans who saddled up their horses and went over just to kill Muslims. They went there in response to a plea for help, because the suffering of the Christians in the Middle East was too great to bear. We must remember how Islam spread to the Middle East. Islam came to the Middle East and conquered with a sword. A sword wielded by Umar the Second Caliph. There was great destruction. So indeed, the Crusades is one of the few times that Kafirs turned to help other Kafirs who were being attacked by jihad.

THE OTHER JIHAD

We have said that jihad is incumbent upon all Muslims. Yet when you go to work, if there's a Muslim who works there he doesn't come in with dynamite strapped to his chest and blow everybody up, but he can still participate in jihad. After 9/11 the FBI started following the money. And it was discovered that many Muslims across the United States were giving quite generously to what are called charities and when the money was given it was understood that it was to support jihad. So when a Muslim writes a check to support jihad he is a jihadist. When a Muslim says "Oh no, no, jihad, holy war, that is not our way. Our way is the religion of peace." That denial is an act of jihad.

The biggest jihad happening in America today is practiced by Saudi Arabia and other Middle East countries. And they're not using the sword, they're using the dollar. The Saudis—Saudi Arabia—spend three times as much money each year as the Soviet Union did to spread communism[2]. What the Saudis are spreading is Islam and Sharia. They pump enormous amounts of money into this country. Most mosques are built with Saudi money, and then staffed by an Imam chosen by the Saudis.

But what is more problematic is the money being spent to affect our politics. Washington, DC is awash in money from the Middle East and this money is used to buy votes, influence people and launch political campaigns. If you're a Muslim and want to run for political office in this country you will not have trouble with financing your campaign. Any Muslim who wants to do anything to advance Islam in this country has

---

2   "Saudi Arabia: Fueling Religious Persecution and Extremism", Nina Shea, delivered before the Religious Freedom Caucus of the US House of Representatives, Dec. 1, 2010
http://www.hudson-ny.org/1717/saudi-arabia-religious-persecution

a blank check. Jihad can be waged with money and the Saudis are using money extensively, just like Mohammed. Mohammed's dying words were these: "Neither Jew or Christian shall be left in Arabia. Keep giving the money to influence the Kafir ambassadors." And that's what the Saudis are doing. They are influencing the Kafir ambassadors and doing it very well.

Another place that Muslims use money to advance jihad is in our educational system. No textbook that teaches about Islam in our schools can be used unless it is approved by a Muslim committee. As a consequence, the only Islam that is studied in our schools is the glorious religion, not a glorious political system. No mention is ever made of the killing of 270 million Kafirs over 1400 years. There is no mention in these textbooks of the dhimmi, a Kafir who is a semi-slave. According to our textbooks, Islam conquered without any suffering at all. No mention is ever made of how Islam has played the key role in slavery for 1400 years. This propaganda that glorifies Islam in our textbooks is jihad. But the educational jihad doesn't stop with textbooks. The Saudis have pumped a large amount of money into our universities' Middle East history departments, Arabic departments, and religion courses. These large amounts of money are to influence how history and religion and politics are taught. Large sums of money are also pumped into professorships supported by the Saudis. Studying Islam in our universities is done with a curriculum that is approved by the Saudis.

So, jihad by the dollar in our education system is far more dangerous than the jihad by sword. Another example of jihad is the fact that anyone in the media who makes a comment will be pressured and threatened with lawsuits. Muslims are using our own civil rights laws with great effect to intimidate and make sure that no one ever says anything about Islam that Muslims don't like. Because you see, freedom of speech is not Sunna, the way of Mohammed.

In the end, it is not the jihad of violence that is so important in our culture. What is important is we do not have any understanding of what is happening. We don't understand that when money is used to influence our politicians, the media and schools, that is jihad. So it is not that Islam is so strong, but that we know so little and that makes us so very, very weak.

Jihad is Islam's strongest political concept. It can be done with the sword, the pen, by the mouth and with money. Mohammed's life furnishes Islam with a perfect example of both tactics and strategy for jihad. The attack on the World Trade Center is a textbook case of jihad, but the most powerful jihad is the Islamification of our civilization.

THE JEWS

ISLAM IS BUILT ON A JEWISH FOUNDATION

Mohammed used the Jews as the basis for being a prophet. The Jews then became an example of what happens to anyone who resists Political Islam. They were assassinated, robbed, executed, raped, enslaved, kidnapped, became the first dhimmis (semi-slaves) and exiled. All of modern Jew hatred by Muslims was formed by Mohammed.

The Jews are very important in the formation of Islam. It could be said that if there were no Jews there would be no Islam. The reason for this can be found in the Koran. When Mohammed had his first vision, which no one else saw, and when he heard the voices that said that the voice was of the Angel Gabriele. This is important because Gabriele is in the Jewish tradition. From the beginning Mohammed said that his authenticity rested on the fact that he had the same basis as the prophets in the Old Testament. There were no Jews in Mecca when he started telling his story of Noah and Adam and Moses. The characters were the same but the stories were different. For instance in the Jewish scripture, the story of Moses and the Pharaoh is about the release of the Jewish slaves. In the Koran, the story of Moses and the Pharaoh is more about the fact that the Pharaoh would not admit that Moses was a prophet. So the Egyptians were destroyed.

In the story of Noah, the same was true. The reason that Allah destroyed the Earth with water was because men would not believe that he was a prophet of Allah. On and on the stories go. All of them changed to advance the Koran's central argument everyone had to listen and do exactly as the prophet of Allah said. The message of the Koran is the entire world is divided into those who believe Mohammed and those who do not.

If there had been Jews in Mecca they would have said: "wait a minute that's not the way this story really happened." The Koran says that the stories in the Old Testament have been corrupted. Adam, Noah, Moses, David, and Solomon all prophesied that one day would come the final messenger of Allah—Mohammed. But the Jews had destroyed all of those prophecies. The real Jewish scriptures are found in the Koran according to the Koran.

ISLAMIC JEW HATRED TODAY

At first the Jews are seen favorably in the Koran of Mecca. But, listen to what Islam has to say today about the Jews in the modern world. Jew hatred by Muslims is reported frequently in Europe today.

Here are some words from modern Muslim political leaders. A former Turkish Prime Minister in front of crowds has publicly proclaimed that "the Jews are bacteria and like a disease[1]".

In the Islamic world there is a large amount of Jew hatred that is part of daily TV fare. Here are some normal conversations about the Jews:

- Egyptian Cleric Abdallah Samak: The Jews, who slayed the prophets, are known for their "Merciless, Murderous, and Bloodthirsty Nature[2]"
- American Center for Islamic Research President Dr. Sallah Sultan: Jews murder non-Jews and use their blood for Passover matzos[3]
- Egyptian Islamic Researcher Abd Al-Khaleq Al-Sharif: The Jews are the most vile among the creatures of Allah[4]
- Egyptian Cleric Hussam Fawzi Jabar: Hitler was right to do what he did to the Jews[5]

This is a decided contrast to Mohammed in Mecca. In Mecca Mohammed practically claims to be a brother to the Jews. He said that he was the last of the line of the Jewish prophets. What explains this? One explanation for this is that Muslims picked up their Jew hatred from modern Europeans. That it's a remnant of Nazism. Let's examine this further. Let's go back long before modern Europe existed.

MEDIEVAL JEW HATRED

In Spain (early eleventh century) Ibn Hazm said, "They are the filthiest and vilest of peoples, their unbelief horrid, their ignorance abominable."[6]

---

1   http://www.memri.org/report/en/0/0/0/0/0/0/2356.htm
2   http://www.thememriblog.org/antisemitism/blog_personal/en/32404.htm
3   http://www.memri.org/report/en/0/0/0/0/0/51/4099.htm
4   http://www.thememriblog.org/antisemitism/blog_personal/en/29750.htm
5   http://www.thememriblog.org/index.php/en/main_antisemitism.htm?blogSubj=antisemitism/&page=7
6   Perlmann, "Eleventh-Century Andalusian Authors of the Jews of Grenada", pg. 279-80.

In Turkey in 1836, "It is impossible to express the contemptuous hatred in which the Turks hold the Jewish people."[7]

In Iran Jews were forced to convert to Islam in the 16th century:

...they were drawn from their quarters on Friday evening into the hills around the city and, after torture, 350 Jews are said to have been forced to convert to Islam. Their synagogues were closed and the Jews were lead to the Mosque, where they had to proclaim publicly the confession of faith, after which a Mullah instructed the newly-converted Muslims in the Koran and practice. These newly converted Muslims had to break with their Jewish past, to allow their daughters to be married to Muslims.[8]

In medieval Iran, a Jew was forbidden to go out into the rain since the water might fall off of him onto the ground and a Muslim might step in it and become contaminated. When it rained, Jews were not allowed in the marketplace.

CLASSICAL JEW HATRED

All of these stories were before there were any of the modern European states, so we have to look elsewhere for the attitudes of Jew hatred by Muslims. Let's go back to the Koran because there are two Korans. The second Koran written in Medina draws a totally different picture of the Jews. There were a lot of Jews in Medina. There were three tribes and they comprised about half the population. When Mohammed entered Medina it did not take long for the Jews to inform him that he was not a prophet in their lineage. No one could contradict Mohammed, so it didn't take long until he took care of the problem. After about a year he had become politically powerful enough to attack one of the Jewish tribes. He beat them and took all of their money and exiled them from Medina. Not long after that, he found an excuse to attack the second Jewish tribe. After he captured them he took all of their wealth and exiled them and took all of their money.

His third attack was against the strongest tribe of Jews. After the Jews surrendered the men were separated from the women and children. The men were taken into the marketplace and one by one their heads were cut off, all 800. Mohammed sat there throughout the day watching alongside 12-year-old wife Aisha. The executions went on into the night by 10

---

7   Julia Pardoe, *The City of the Sultan and Domestic Manners of the Turks in 1836*, pg. 167-68.

8   Andrew Bostom, *The Legacy of Islamic Antisemitism*, pg. 133.

o'clock at night the last Jew lost his head by torchlight. The Jewish children were adopted in the Muslim families and raised as Muslims. He sold the women in wholesale lots into slavery.[1] This is a story that every Muslim knows.

After the Jews of Medina had been destroyed Mohammed did not stop there. He went north to Khaybar where the Jews were prosperous. He put them under siege and after they surrendered, he took all of their wealth. But this time he did not kill them. A dead Jew does not make you any money. He created a new form of human being called the dhimmi. A dhimmi existed in a completely Islamic world. A Jew could only be Jewish in his home or in the synagogue. All of the culture, laws and politics was Islamic. A dhimmi had to pay a tax, the jizya. Half of everything they earned was paid to Islam and Mohammed. The Koran says in addition to paying the tax that the dhimmi has to be humiliated.

Three years after that when Umar was caliph, that is supreme ruler of all of Islam, he drove the Jews out of Arabia. From that day forward there have been no Jews in Arabia. Saudi Arabia exists in religious apartheid.

The Koran goes further in talking about the Jews; it calls them apes. Remember, earlier back when the fatwa ruled that the Jews are apes and pigs? The modern scholar wasn't making that up. Mohammed added further that the Jews were rats. So we have two totally different views of the Jews. This is dualism. One view of the Jews is that the Jews and Muslims worship the same God. Why, they are brothers. The other view of the Jews is that they are apes and rats. These are two opposite ideas, but due to dualism inside of Islam they are both true. A Muslim can say to the Jew, "We worship the same God. We are brothers in religion." Or he can say they're apes and rats.

MODERN JEW HATRED

Let's move forward from Medina to modern times. There is a problem between Jews and Muslims today. It's known as the Israeli-Palestinian conflict. It is important to know that it is the official position of the Israeli government that Islam plays no part in the problem of Israel. Let's listen to what the leaders of the Palestinians say. Here is one leader. "I support the Palestinian cause. I support jihad." Israelis proclaim that the problem is simply a modern political problem. It is a struggle between nation states, but jihad is not a modern concept. It is a 1400-year-old concept.

---

1 *The Life of Muhammad*, A. Guillaume, Oxford University Press, Karachi, 1982, pgs. 464-466.

A leader of Hamas said: "the Koran used terms that are closer to animals than human beings. The Jews were likened to a donkey carrying books and were compared to apes and pigs. The Israelis today are the descendents of apes and pigs". Another leader said: "the Prophet Mohammed foretold that Judgment Day would come only when the Muslims fight the Jews and the Muslims would kill the Jews and the stones and trees would say "servant of Allah there is a Jew behind me. Come and kill him."

Another Islamic leader says: Allah willing we will enter Israel as conquerors and liberators, not through negotiations, but through jihad.

We have two very different views of the problem in Israel. Jews today deny that Islam has anything to do with Israel's problem. While Muslims say that Islam demands that jihad will annihilate Israel.

We've covered the history of Jews in Islam and saw that Mohammed enslaved, killed and created the dhimmi. In that one word, dhimmi, we find the reason that Jews and Christians do not recognize the source of their problems in Islam. They have been annihilated, humiliated and shamed. Jews and Christians were dhimmis. Whether it was North Africa, Spain, Turkey or Egypt, the dhimmis were treated badly. No one wants to remember such dreadful history, so they deny its existence.

LIES

Instead of telling this 1400-year history of shame, Jewish scholars create a beautiful lie, the lie of the Golden Age of Islam. It is said that the high point of civilization was found in Islamic Spain. It was a culture of tolerance and in great intellectual striving. There is a wee bit of truth to this, in that there were a few Jews and a few Christians who prospered and were in high places of government as advisers and in other capacities. But to call this a golden age is an elitist view, because there were very few who prospered. Can a golden age exist that is based upon the dhimmitude of Kafirs? Can it be a golden age when the Europeans fought for seven hundred years to drive out Islam from Spain? Can a Jewish scholar call the history a golden age when 4000 Jews[2] were killed in one day in Granada? There may have been some gold flecks in Spain but it was no golden age. So it is the history of the dhimmi that explained the amnesia about the history of Islam and the Jews. The history is too bad. No Kafir wants to look back and see that his ancestors were enslaved. No Jew wants to look back and see that for 1400 years they were dirt on the street in Islam.

---

2   *The Legacy of Islamic Antisemitism,* Andrew Bostom, Prometheus Books, 2008, pg. 24.

It is sad that this history is not remembered. Until Israel sees its true place in history, that the Jews of Israel are descendents of the dhimmis of Islam; until Jews accept that the real struggle is jihad, they will be doomed to repeat the history of Khaybar. The only way to save Israel is to see the true history of Islam. Living a lie of denial of the history of Islam is not a way to preserve Israel.

THE CHRISTIANS

Islam has two views of Christians (duality again). The first view is that Christianity and Islam are brother religions. The second view is that Christians must change their religion to meet the demands of Islam. Modern Christians want to believe that there is a bridge between Islam and Christianity. But the history of Islam shows that Islam first deceives and then annihilates Christianity. For 1400 years Islam has destroyed Christian lands.

The Christians do not play a pivotal role like the Jews did in the formation of Islam. That is, the Koran does not have a lot to say about Christians. Nor does the Sira, the life of Mohammed, have much to say about Christians. But Islam's attitude towards the Christians can be seen in some of the final days of Mohammed's life when he sent out troops against the Christians in the North of Syria. So it was Mohammed's intent to attack the Christians. Soon after he died that's what happened. The Christians played a very important role in historical Islam because all the Middle East, North Africa, and what we now call Turkey was Christian.

MODERN CHRISTIAN DHIMMITUDE

Since these areas are Islamic today, there is a history there but let's take a look at Islam through a much more modern eye. Soon after 9/11, the Muslims started going out to churches to speak to Christians about Islam, the peaceful religion. Well one church decided to go that one better[1]. They invited a group of imams (the imams are Muslim religious leaders) and they also invited several Christian ministers. The Christians arrived that night in ones and twos. Then about the time the meeting was to start, in came all the Muslims. The imams came in as a group onto the stage and the Muslim men filed in next. They surrounded the Christians in their seats. And then the Muslim women came in all dressed in black from head to toe, and they sat in the back of the room. As Muslim women, they knew what their place was in public gatherings.

---

1   This event was personally attended in 2002 by the author.

The first thing that happened was an imam walked up to the lectern and placed a very large Koran on top and opened it up about half way. This was a symbolic act that was indicative of the entire night. The Christians didn't think anything about it one way or the other, but for the Muslims, it was a mark of who they were.

You see, Islam is a word that means submission. This word submission has several meanings. For the Muslim it means to submit to the Koran, the will of Allah and the Sunna of Mohammed. And, all Muslims are to make all others who are not Muslims submit to them. They were there to dominate. What the Muslims did was to place the Koran as the focal point of dominance because this is where the Bible would have been. This act of dominance was symbolic of the night.

One of the imams got up and started to give his talk. He first said that Christians and Muslims worship the same God. Well that seemed like a good foot to get started on. Of course this is not true but since the Christians did not know anything about the god Allah that seemed fine to them. The imam went ahead and said they too honor Jesus because Jesus was a prophet of Allah and that Jesus was a Muslim. He also explained that Jesus was not the son of God. He was merely a Muslim Prophet. And for that matter, the apostles were also Muslims. This came perhaps as a surprise to the ministers but they didn't say anything. The imam then went ahead to say that Jesus was not crucified, therefore was not resurrected.

The next thing he told the Christians was that the concept of the Trinity was a great affront to Allah. There was no such thing as the Trinity and that it made the Christians polytheist. The fact that the Christians are viewed as polytheist explains something that happened at the beginning when the minister first said let us pray together. There was almost a panicked response from the imams at this. "No," they said, "we do not pray with others." This was quite puzzling to the Christian minister but since the Christians were there as hosts and they were there to be kind and polite, he didn't say anything. But not knowing anything about Islam, you can tell from the puzzled look on the minister's face, why would they object to praying together? The reason is that the Christians are viewed as polytheists. To pray with them is a terrible sin, so terrible that it has a special name, shirk. The Koran says that if they had prayed with the Christians, they would definitely go to Hell. Praying with the Christians would have been a sin worse than mass murder.

Again the Christians did not understand anything about Islam or they would have never made the invitation to prayer. Or they would have simply prayed while the Muslims were setting there. The Muslims dominated on this point. Inside the Christian Church, there would be no prayers with the Christians.

Another thing that the imam said in his talk was that the New Testament was a corrupt document and was in error. Not only was the New Testament in error so was the Old Testament. But in particular, the reason that the New Testament was wrong was that the prophet of Allah, Jesus' chief prophecy was that after him would come the final prophet and his name would be Ahmed. (Ahmed and Mohammed is like Bill and William) The imam said Christians had removed these prophecies from the New Testament. This was one of the many reasons that the New Testament was a document which was simply wrong. If Christians wanted to learn the real story of Jesus they would have to read the Koran, because the Koran contains the exact truth about Isa, the Arabic word for Jesus.

CHRISTIAN IGNORANCE

Imagine if the Christian minister had stood up and made these assertions—that Mohammed was not a prophet of any sort, that the Koran was a derivative work, that is it was just a book in which things were copied from the Jews and Christians, Zorastrians and the old Arabic religions, that Allah was simply the tribal moon god of the Quraysh tribe. That is equivalent to what the Muslim minister said but Christians didn't do that for two reasons. One, they were the host and they were going to be nice. The other reason was they had no idea that the Koran was a derivative work. In response to questions from the audience, none of the Christians had read the Koran nor had they read the traditions of Mohammed, the Hadith. Nor did they know anything about Mohammed's life. But, the imams had read the New Testament and the Old Testament. So they knew the Christians and the Christians knew nothing of them. This was the way the entire night went. The Christians were asked questions by the Muslims and the questions that they asked were 1400 years old. These were stock questions but the ministers were caught flat-footed. They had never thought about these kinds of questions before. Again the Muslims came prepared and the Christians were not prepared.

The lack of preparation by the Christians could be shown when one minister started talking badly about the Crusades and apologized for them. This meant he knew nothing about the Crusades. Yes, mistakes were made in the Crusades, but overall, they were a great good. And why were they a great good? It was one of the few times the Christians in Europe recognized the intense suffering of the Christians in the Middle East. The reasons the Crusades were started were simple. They came as a response to a cry for help. And why did these Christians cry for help? Because they were being murdered, robbed and taxed to death by their Muslim overlords.

Now how did these Muslims become their overlords? Because originally that part of the world had been mostly Christian. It did not become Islamic because some imams showed up and started preaching in the marketplace. No. It was Islamic because the sword had been used to kill all those who would defend Christianity and to take over the government. The Crusaders arrived in response to a desperate cry for help.

Basically the minister with his comments said he didn't know anything about the history of Christianity and Islam. This is tragic, dreadfully tragic. For over 60 million Christians have been killed in the process of jihad. How did Turkey which is 99.7 percent Islamic go from a Greek culture, a country called Anatolia, how did that country go from being Christian to Islamic? The Christians on the stage didn't know how this process happened or know that 60 million Christians have died in jihad. They also didn't know that in the 20th century alone a million Armenians were killed in Turkey. Why didn't the ministers know these dreadful facts? Very simply, it's because they went to divinity school and no one ever mentioned these facts. They had never been taught the doctrine of Islam. They didn't know, for instance, that Islam is primarily a political ideology, not a religion.

EDUCATION

Why don't they teach this at the universities and divinity schools? Nothing happens by accident. And in this case, the reason that Christians don't teach the history of Christianity and Islam is this. The history is so dreadful, so painful, it could even be called disgusting.

Islam has a political status for the Christians called a dhimmi. The Jews were the first dhimmis but the Christians were the biggest dhimmis of all for one simple reason. There were far more of them. When the Muslims came in and took over the government and implemented Islamic law, Sharia law, part of this was how Christians and Jews would be treated in public and how they would be treated in the courts of law. It was dreadful. A dhimmi has no civil rights. So this history of dhimmitude and special taxes that Christians had to pay was dreadfully humiliating.

It's a shameful history that includes the death of 60 million Christians. None of the Christians up on the stage knew what happened to the seven churches of Asia. In the book of Revelation in the New Testament, the Seven Churches are addressed. The Seven Churches were in Asia minor which was Anatolia or what we call Turkey today. They don't know what happened to those churches which is a real tragedy, because in the destruction of those churches is the history of Islam.

And Christians also had not studied enough about Islam to know that not only had 60 million Christians been killed in jihad but 80 million Hindus, 10 million Buddhists and 120 million Africans[1].

The Christians up on the stage that day didn't know enough to ask about slavery. Because you see, every slave that was sold to the white man was bought from a Muslim wholesaler. The Christians didn't know enough to ask why is it that when you say the Arabic word for African, *abd*, it's the same word that's used for a black slave. This night was a demonstration of two things, the knowledge and power of Islam and how the Christians have not done their homework.

Christians and all Kafirs should know how to use the golden rule to attack the Koran. Christians and all Kafirs should know the story of Mohammed.

All Kafirs should know enough about the Koran that when a Muslim says Christians, Jews and Muslims worship the same God, that you offer arguments to show how that simply is not true.

All Kafirs, not just Christians, should be able to debate on the issue of Political Islam, if not with a Muslim, then with someone at work or wherever else. What actual argument can anybody make for being ignorant about the history of Political Islam?

The dreadful history of Islam is moving through our world today. As an example, Iraq which used to have a Christian majority is now only 5% Christian[2]. Why is it that they're being persecuted? In Africa, Christian Africans are being killed and destroyed almost on a daily basis. How can these people be helped?

What is done to Christians is done to Hindus, Buddhists and atheists. Islam does not discriminate. All Kafirs must submit.

If you're aware of the history of Islam, if you're aware of its political doctrine, then you can be more useful in the debate about the true nature of Islam. And knowledge about Islam is not merely an ability to hold forth in public debate. Knowledge about Islam will sensitize you so that your

---

1   http://www.politicalislam.com/tears/pages/tears-of-jihad/

2   Hearings in Washington about attacks against christians of Iraq and Egypt by Gary Feuerberg,Epoch Times Staff, Jan, 26, 2011
http://www.christiansofiraq.com/hearingaboutattacks-againstchristiansof-iraqandegypt.html

politics change, so that you can see that not only has Islam killed 270 million Kafirs in the past, but it's doing so today.

Kafir civilization is being destroyed on a daily basis by Islam. The way to prevent this destruction is very simple. We must arm ourselves with knowledge about Islamic history, knowledge about the Koran and Mohammed.

THE DHIMMI

Dhimmis lives in fear of Islam but agrees that they will not resist Political Islam and they will even support it. In return dhimmis can live safely. Dhimmitude is in the mind of the dhimmi. Today we see our politicians, journalists and intellectuals play the role of dhimmis.

The dhimmi was a unique invention by Mohammed. He created a new type of creature and that creature is a semi-slave. Dhimmis started with what Mohammed did to the Jews. He took their land and then let them work the land and paid a tax, the jizya, that was half of their income. A dhimmi was a Kafir who lived under Islamic, Sharia, law. The first dhimmis were the Jews, but Christians and others were added later.

Jews and Christians could still practice their religion but that must be done in a private way. The laws were Islamic; the dress was dictated by Islamic law. A dhimmi was not really free. For instance a church couldn't ring its bells because bells are a sign of Satan, according to Mohammed. A dhimmi couldn't hold any job that made him a supervisor over Muslims. This limited rank in the military. If Christians wanted to repair the church, or Jews the synagogue, they had to get permission from the government. All of these laws are dreadful because they established a second-class citizenship; the dhimmi did not have civil rights. A dhimmi couldn't sue a Muslim or prosecute a crime against a Muslim. Usually, when the Christian or the Jewish dhimmi came to pay their yearly jizya tax, they were humiliated—grabbed by the beard, slapped in the face, or made to kneel and give the money. They were humiliated because the Koran said to humiliate the dhimmi.

In some Islamic countries, particularly when the country felt powerful, it was more tolerant towards the dhimmis. A dhimmi could even rise to a decent level of power within government, but that could all vanish overnight. The treatment of the dhimmi was shown in Coptic Egypt. (the Copts were the original Egyptians.) A dhimmi could have his tongue removed if he spoke Coptic in front of an Islamic government official. The dhimmi was always persecuted and was never really an equal.

When the Egyptian military tried to conquer the Byzantine Christians, but lost a battle, back in Egypt the Muslims rioted against the Christians. Christians would be killed because riots were one of the favorite ways to punish the dhimmi. When Smyrna—the last of the seven churches of Asia—was destroyed in 1922, it was not done with the military and bulldozers. No, rioting Muslims did it. Riots are a form of jihad. The dhimmi could always be persecuted, not only in the courts of law, but a riot could destroy an entire section of a city. Dhimmis were killed if they criticized Mohammed, and actually dhimmis were not even supposed to study Mohammed at all.

TREATY OF UMAR

There was a formal treaty called the Treaty of Umar, which laid out everything that was to be done to the dhimmi. A dhimmi could not ride a horse, but he could ride an ass or a donkey. If they were caught on a horse, they could be pulled off and beaten. When a dhimmi met a Muslim on the sidewalk, he had to step out into the street and let the Muslim pass. The dhimmi also had to wear special clothing or, if not special clothing, a belt or a patch on the clothing to immediately identify a person as a dhimmi. The only protection that a Christian or a Jew had would be to make Muslim friends because many times the Muslim friend could keep the weight of dhimmi laws off of his Christian or Jewish friend.

The persecution of the dhimmis was unrelenting. It went on for generation after generation. Finally the dhimmi would give up and become a Muslim. All of a sudden he had more money because he didn't have to pay the jizya tax. Converted dhimmis could be promoted in their jobs. They would not be spit at or have stones thrown at them on the street. They could go to court and be treated as full, equal citizens.

As the centuries passed, more and more dhimmis converted to Islam. Dhimmitude, which is the mind of the dhimmi, destroys the civilization because the only way out is by giving up all of your old culture. When Islam moved into Coptic Egypt, the culture was a blend of the old pharonic culture mixed with the culture of the Greeks. In the end all of the Coptic culture disappeared just as the pyramids were stripped of their beautiful marble veneer. Why? Because Islam's goal is to destroy all Kafir civilization.

ANNIHILATION

Islam seeks to annihilate all other cultures by the dhimmi laws that come out of the Sharia, Islamic law. The lack of civil rights, the abuse, humiliation and tax burden wears away the spirit to resist becoming Islamic. They get new names and names of cities change and then the cultural history vanishes. Once a nation has been fully Islamisized, all of its history disappears. When Napoleon invaded Egypt, none of the Muslims there could explain anything about the old temples, the statues, or the pyramids. The people were ignorant of their history. They didn't remember anything because the culture of the pharaohs had been annihilated. The culture of the Greeks in Anatolia was destroyed. In Pakistan, a Muslim country, the native culture was Hindu. Afghanistan was a Buddhist culture that has been completely annihilated.

Part of the Islamic takeover and eradication of a nation and its culture is the destruction of sacred sites. Churches or temples that are beautiful or valuable were converted to mosques. At one time an estimate put the number of churches destroyed by the Islamic conquest of Turkey near 20,000. India had magnificent temples of worship which the Muslims destroyed.

Islam invented defacing. When Islam invaded a country, all of the religious objects were destroyed just as Mohammed destroyed all religious art. If there was a mural on a wall, the face was destroyed. Once the face was gone, the rest of the object was left. The Sphinx does not have a nose because it was defaced by Muslims.

The purpose of dhimmitude was twofold: (1) to bring in money by the dhimmi tax and (2) to slowly grind out the dhimmi's culture. This process worked really well. As a matter of fact, it was so successful that there is a black hole in all of history about dhimmitude. No one studies this part of world history. As a result, today in our universities the history of the dhimmi is not taught and is never mentioned. In some divinity schools, which consider themselves sophisticated, the dhimmi is discussed. However, what is said is, "Oh, the dhimmi was protected." It makes life as a dhimmi sound warm and fuzzy like living in the arms of your father. And the question arises: protected from what and whom? What is not taught is how the dhimmi was humiliated. When it is said that the dhimmi was protected, it is the truth. To be protected as a dhimmi means that as long as one kept paying the tax he would not be killed nor would his goods be stolen, unless there was a riot. In a riot no dhimmi was protected.

Today there is no Islamic country strong enough to have a full legal dhimmi or slavery as a formal policy. However, both the dhimmi and slavery are part of Islam and Sharia law, and the doctrine of Islam cannot be changed. For every Muslim the Koran is complete, perfect and absolute. The condition and rule of the dhimmi is laid out in the Koran, so the dhimmi cannot be eliminated. The reason that there is no longer a formal dhimmi status is that Islam is not powerful enough to enforce it. Instead of having a formal status for the dhimmi, bigotry and prejudice limit the civil rights. This leads to extralegal persecution of Kafirs.

DHIMMITUDE

Dhimmitude is the attitude of one who always tries to placate the bully. Islam is always pressuring for this attitude of submission. For example, the Sharia, Islamic law, permits a Muslim to have up to four wives. In the West we have monogamy laws. However, England allows a Muslim to bring in more than one wife, and they all can qualify for welfare. This is dhimmitude. Dhimmitude is submitting to Islam for the simple purpose of submitting.

Another example of dhimmitude is the phrase "the war on terror." The war on terror is the mark of a dhimmi because it does not name the enemy. After Pearl Harbor the United States did not declare war against the kamikazes. It named the enemy and declared war against Japan. Dhimmis don't want to have a ideological war against Political Islam. Thus, we create an artificial phrase that has no meaning. "Terror" is a technique. We cannot go to war against a technique; we only can go to war against an enemy.

We see dhimmitude in government in hiring and promotion. Government agencies give preference to Muslim Arabs over Christian Arabs in translation work. Forums are opened for Muslims to come in and talk about Islam. As a contrary example, Buddhists do not get a forum to explain Buddhism.

The United States prides itself on freedom of the press and political speech. Citizens are supposed to have the right to stand up and say anything about politics. People might laugh at you, and they may not vote for you, but it's not a crime to speak. Remember the Mohammed cartoons? What newspaper in the United States published the Mohammed cartoons? Mohammed was a political figure and yet our newspapers, by law having freedom of the press, did not publish those cartoons. Newspapers defended themselves, saying that they did not want to offend anyone. Politics frequently necessitates offending someone. Newspapers are in the business of offending people at times. The newspapers were not offending Islam to be nice, but because dhimmis are always afraid of Islam. Dhimmis are always looking for a way to placate and appease. When the cartoons were not shown on TV and when they were not published in the newspapers, those refusals to exercise freedom of speech or freedom of the press were acts of dhimmis. No one was being nice; they were being dhimmis.

To slowly accept Sharia law is another form of dhimmitude. Airports in the United States are changing the plumbing so that Muslims will have a place to wash their feet before prayer[1]. Universities have "meditation rooms," however, the Muslims monopolize them[2]. If a university is questioned about this seemingly unfair use, it will not defend the practice. That is dhimmitude. When a workplace that runs an assembly line says, "If you're Muslim we will provide for you a place to pray, and you can leave the production line when it is prayer time." That's dhimmitude since the dhimmi agrees to this out of fear to placate Islam.

In the United States and in Europe there is no formal dhimmi status, but there is dhimmitude. As a result of this attitude, Europe is rapidly becoming Islamisized. The day will come when the churches in Europe will live in fear, as they do now in Turkey. A churches will have to get permission from the Muslim masters to get the roof fixed. The reason the people will be subject to Islamic rule is that they never studied the history of the dhimmi and never studied the history of Political Islam.

The people who do not study the history of Political Islam and do not study the history of the dhimmi and learn from it are doomed to repeat the subjection of the dhimmis and lose their civilization.

---

1   World Net Daily, April 28, 2007 http://www.wnd.com/?pageId=43815
2   Inside Higher Ed, "Meditation Room or Mosque" January 2008 http://www.insidehighered.com/news/2008/01/03/meditation

WOMEN

The dualism of Islam allows for two ways to treat women. They can be honored and protected or they can be beaten. Today Western nations allow Islamic women to be treated as Islam wants to treat them. In short, they are not subject to our laws and customs of equality. Why? Our politicians and intellectuals do not want to offend Islam by discussing the second class status of women in Islam.

DOCTRINE

If you're going to study Islam you have to study women as a separate category. And the reason for this is simple—Islamic doctrine denies that men and women are equal. The dualism of Islam separates women into a separate category. The Koran has whole sections devoted to how women are treated differently from men. Many hadith show women as a special category. Islam is very proud of how it treats its women and says that in the West our treatment of women is terrible, that they are not protected and honored. In Islam, they say that women are protected and honored.

Let's examine the doctrine that underlies each separate case of how women are treated. Islam is a rational system of politics and culture. It always has a doctrinal reason for everything it does and this is one of the things that makes studying Islam easy. If Muslims do it, there is a reason. It doesn't need to create a reason, because Islam has a perfect, universal and final doctrine. Islam even claims that it is the world's first feminist movement—that after Islam women had more rights than before.

Let's examine the subject of beatings. The Koran is clear. It says that if a woman does not obey her husband—that is, does not submit—she can be beaten. Let's see how this plays out. In Germany an imam who preaches about peace and interfaith issues was arrested for wife-beating. His wife's nose and shoulder were broken. As the imam beat her he keep repeating a Koran verse justifying beating a wife. The woman had born one of his ten children. She wanted to live a more Western life-style. His last lecture was about an Islam that distances itself from violence.[1]

PRACTICE

At the border between Pakistan and Afghanistan, it was decided that everyone who crossed the border had to be photographed. The US military was doing this and since many of the people coming across the border were Afghani women in their full head-to-toe burqa—including the face veil—they were taken to a separate tent where a female soldier helped them get their burqa off and photographed their face.

Now this is merely anecdotal information that was passed to me by a soldier, and doesn't have any scientific evidence, but the women who did this work said that it seemed to them like nine out of ten women that they saw had been bruised in the face.

This goes along with what the Pakistan Institute of Medical Science reported. In a scientific survey of Pakistani women, about 90% of them said that they had been beaten by their husbands. In the country of Chad, in Africa, they tried to outlaw beatings, but Islam is quite strong in Chad. The imams and other Islamic leaders protested, saying that anti-wife beating laws were against Sharia law. The bill was defeated.

Some argue cynically, but practically, that since Islamic women are beaten from early on, by the time they are married they are used to this treatment and it does not seem to bother them. This business of beating wives is thoroughly established in Islam. This is not some sort of aberration. We've already mentioned that the Koran says that the beating of a wife is permitted. It also goes further to say, though, that if the woman submits she should be given food, clothing and shelter, so those are also part of a woman's rights.

MOHAMMED

Mohammed left behind a great deal of information about the beating of women. There is one tradition which summarizes Islam and women. He said never ask a man why he beats his wife. We know that from one tradition (hadith) that he himself hit his favorite wife, Aisha, and we know that he stood by without comment when her father struck Aisha in his presence. But then again, Mohammed also stood by without saying a word

---

1   http://www.dailymail.co.uk/news/article-1335024/Muslim-imam-Sheikh-Adam-lectures-non-violence-arrested-wife-beating.html?ito=feeds-newsxml

when Ali beat Aisha's black female slave. Ali was Mohammed's cousin, son-in-law and the fourth caliph (supreme leader).

There's a famous hadith[1] where a woman comes to Mohammed with a complaint about her husband. The hadith says that there was a bruise on her face which was green in color. Mohammed addressed the issue that she brought up, but he made no remark about the bruise on her face. Actually, at another time he left a hadith which said that when you hit women, do not strike them in the face. He also left behind one other piece of information on the beating of women. He said that they should be beaten lightly. This invites questions. What does it mean to beat lightly? Does it mean to use a small stick? And to use a stick, can you raise the stick above the head as you strike down at the woman? The Sunna doesn't describe this, it merely says that they are to be beaten lightly.

Now Islam is a dualistic system. Dualism means that Islam always has two contradictory positions. So if there is a statement that says that it is proper to beat a woman, then somewhere else there will be a contradictory statement. So, in another hadith, Mohammed said: "Do not strike Allah's handmaidens." That is, don't hit women. However, there are only one or two of these statements and there are many which describe how women should be subjugated. Of course, in Islam hitting a woman is not abuse because hitting a woman is allowed and not forbidden. If she's been trained properly she does not object to these beatings. Since Mohammed established very firmly that striking women was within the bounds of Islam, Sharia incorporates the Sunna of Mohammed into the formal structure of Islamic law.

There are rules laid out as to the gradation of how the man makes the woman submit and the final stage is a beating. Now let's look at another way that women are treated. In 2002, researchers in refugee camps in Afghanistan and Pakistan found that half the girls were married by age 13.[2] In an Afghan refugee camp more than two out of three second grade girls were either married or engaged! Virtually all the girls who were beyond second grade were already married. One ten-year-old was engaged to a man of 60. Fifty-seven percent of Afghan girls under the age of 16 and

---

1 *The Submission of Women and Slaves*, CSPI Publishing, pg. 56.

2 Andrew Bushell, "Child Marriage in Afghanistan and Pakistan," America, March 11, 2002, p. 12 from the "Violent Oppression of Women in Islam", Robert Spencer and Phyllis Chesler, Frontpage Magazine PDF, pg. 15. http://frontpagemag.com/upload/pamphlets/ViolentOpp.pdf

many as young as nine, are in arranged marriages.[3] This is pure Sunna, the way of Mohammed. How do we know this? When Mohammed was in his mid-fifties, he was engaged to Aisha, a child of six. Then, when she was nine years old, he consummated the marriage. So, when the 60-year-old Pakistani Muslim is engaged to the 10-year-old it is Sunna, it is the way of Mohammed.

HONOR KILLINGS

Now we come to a treatment of Islamic women which is not strictly Islamic doctrine, and that is "honor killings." An honor killing is when a man kills a woman because she has violated his honor. A Muslim male must control the sexuality of the females in his household or he is dishonored. It is one of his chief concerns. In Dallas, Texas two Muslim sisters were found shot to death in the back of their father's taxicab. The father is being sought by the police in conjunction with the murder. A friend who knew them said the father was very strict about the girl's relationships with boys, their talking with boys, as well as the type of clothing the daughters wore. The sisters dressed in Western clothes and listened to popular music. The father was quite angry that his daughters were not acting like proper Muslim women.[4] Islam does not say kill the woman who does not obey. Instead, it brings the level of punishment up to beatings. However, once a woman can be subjugated and beaten, it's not too far from taking the final step. Killing a family member over the issue of Islam is Sunna. We know at the Battle of Badr there is a story in which a son is remorseful about having killed his father, who was a Kafir, but in the end he realizes that since his father was a Kafir, even though he was a cultured man, it was better that he was dead. So it is Sunna for one family member to kill another to advance Islam.

RIGHTS

The Koran speaks at great length about women's rights. Among them are these: that they are to receive half the amount of inheritance of a male, and that in a court of law it takes the testimony of two women to equal the

---

3 "Harmful Traditional Practices and Implementation of the Law On Elimination of Violence Against Women in Afghanistan", UNAMA & OHCHR, Pgs., 18-21. December 9, 2010. http://unama.unmissions.org/Portals/UNAMA/Publication/HTP%20REPORT_ENG.pdf
4 "Honor Killing in Dallas", Canada Free Press, January 8, 2008. http://www.canadafreepress.com/index.php/article/1255

testimony of one man. So, if a woman testifies against a man and he denies the accusation, then the testimony has no weight at all. In Islamic court this makes cases of rape almost impossible to prove.

Muslims will say: "Oh no, no, no! Islam teaches the equality of women!" and indeed, there are many verses which say that women are equal on Judgment Day. That's when they're equal. Then every person will be called upon to account for what they did and said in life, and in this matter men and women are to be treated equally.

Let's examine the fine print. It is true that the Koran says that women are to be treated equally on Judgment Day. They are to be judged on what they did in this life, and what they're supposed to do in this life is to obey the men, to submit to them, therefore, their "equality" on Judgment Day means that they will be judged on how well they submitted to men.

Mohammed commented that he had seen Hell and the great majority of its inhabitants were women. Why were they there? They had not fully appreciated their husbands. In the same hadith, he made the remark that women were spiritually inferior to men and that women were not as intelligent as men. Part of a woman's "rights" inside of Islam is that she's not as intelligent and she has a much better chance of going to Hell.

But even if she goes to Paradise, she is still in for second-class treatment. Paradise for men is a sexual playground, but none of that seems to extend to women, so that even in Paradise, women are not rewarded like men.

There's another interesting comment about women and worship in Islam. A man is to pray facing Mecca, the women are to be behind him in prayer. This is the reason why women always sit in the back in the mosque. Now it's interesting in the religion of Islam there are many things which can negate the power of prayer. One of those is if while you're praying a dog, a donkey or a woman should walk in front of you. So for the purposes of this tradition a woman is equal to a dog or a donkey.

THE VEIL AND OTHER RULES OF SUBJUGATION

Now let's take up the matter of the infamous burqa—the covering from head-to-toe which can even include the face. Some Islamic women say "Well, that is not really required." Others say that it is. So on this issue the Koran displays a dualism. We do know this: Mohammed made all of his wives wear a veil, and that everyone in the entourage around him did so. So although there is not a universal commandment that says women should wear a burqa, we do know that from the Sunna of Mohammed, his wives did that and all the women around him did. This is a powerful influence over modern Islam.

In the Muslim holy city of Mecca, a girls' school caught on fire[1]. Naturally, the girls tried to escape, but they were driven back into the burning building because they were not wearing their face covering and full-body veil. They died because it was the decision of the religious police that better they should die than have their faces exposed in the public.

Another aspect of Islam is polygamy. The Koran is quite clear on polygamy. A man have one, two, three or four wives. It does not say that a woman can have one, two, three, or four husbands.

There is also the matter of stoning. Now it can be argued that stoning is not Islamic, or it can be argued that it is Islamic. Here's a situation in Tehran, Iran which calls itself an Islamic republic. In 2008, two sisters, Zohre and Azar Kabiri, were convicted of adultery. They were sentenced to be stoned to death, because adultery is a crime punishable by death. At first they were convicted of having illegal relations with men and they were given 99 lashings each. They were brought back into court and the same evidence was used to try them for adultery, whereupon they were sentenced to be stoned to death. The evidence? It was a videotape where the two sisters were caught talking to some men without adult family members with them.[2] The same event, two women talking to two men, was used to fires beat and then kill two women.

There's an interesting thing about stoning, by the way. Sharia law is very technical about this, and what it says is that the stones should be chosen so they do not kill immediately. They have to be big enough so that when enough of them are thrown, they will kill the victim. Death by stoning is meant to be a torturous death that the entire community participates in.

OUR FAILURE

Now we come to an important thing. We have just described Islam. We must now talk about our response to this, and our response to this is shameful. In this country, starting in the 1960s, we had a political movement called

---

1   "Saudi Police Stop Fire Rescue" BBC, March 15, 2002, http://news.bbc.co.uk/2/hi/1874471.stm
2   "Equality Now Calls on Iran to Stop the Imminent Execution of Iranian Sisters Zohreh and Azar Kabiri Recently Sentenced to Death by Stoning for Adultery" http://www.equalitynow.org/english/pressroom/rapid_response_alert/rra_iran_en.html
"Two Sisters Zohre and Azar Kabiri Face Death By Stoning" Iran Human Rights, English, February 5, 2008. http://iranhr.net/spip.php?article196

feminism which said women should be fully equal to men before the law, and a great deal of progress has been made in that. But on the issue of Islam, Kafir women are shamefully silent. What we see here is an indication of how our universities, for instance, have responded to Islam. They are silent. Universities should be a place where issues are discussed and described but where is their a single Women's Studies department that teach about Sharia law about women in Islam? Social workers do not report beatings inside Islamic families in Europe. The whole system has turned a blind eye to this.

What's happening in Europe—and it's starting to happen in America—is this: Muslim civil rights organizations maintain that Muslims should not fall under any aspect of family law in the West because our family law is based on ignorance of Allah's law. Therefore, there should be two sets of laws—one for Kafirs and one for Muslims. So if a beaten Muslim woman shows up at the emergency room, the police would not be called. Or if she wishes to press charges, it would be in an Islamic court.

What is the response of Western women to this? Well, they don't want to be culturally insensitive. They don't want to be racist. So, if this culture of Islam wants to beat its women, why should they say anything about it? Our universal human rights stop at Mohammed's door.

Islam has a precise doctrine of how to treat women. Other than after death, the Islamic treatment of women is that they are less than a man. That is dreadful, but what is worse is that we will not help Islamic women for fear we will offend Islam.

SLAVERY

You do not know the history of slavery if you do not know about Islam and slavery. Slavery is very important and is part of a highly developed doctrine in Islam. It has a 1400 year old history which is still alive today in Africa. Mohammed was a slave owner and trader who dealt in every aspect of slavery.

It is impossible to study the history of Mohammed and the beginnings of Islam and not become involved in the role of slavery. Some people think that slavery only happened when white men showed up in wooden ships off the coast of Africa, went into the bush, captured slaves and brought them back to sell in America. That is the generally accepted history of slavery in America.

That does contain an element of truth but it's not remotely the story of world slavery, or even how slave trading worked in the Americas.

To study slavery from the standpoint of the world, you must study Islam because Islam has enslaved all others—the African, the European, the Asian—they have enslaved everybody.

SLAVERY TODAY

Francis Bok, a Christian, appeared at a university to give a talk. It was very interesting because he was an actual freed African slave. He and his sister had gone to the market to sell beans and while they were in the market place, Muslim jihadis showed up. They captured his sister and him along with others and set out on a forced march. Every night his sister was raped by the members of the troop. When they finally got to the jihadis' camp, they were put on the block and sold as slaves. Once Francis was sold, he was taken to the new master's home. He was placed in the center of the family and every member of the family took a small stick and began to beat him with it. Then they informed him that he no longer had any name. From this day forward there was no more Francis Bok. There was only abd, black slave.

Now this is interesting. Abd is an Arabic word but it's only one of about forty different words that Islam has for slave. That's very interesting because in the English language we simply have one word—slave. Now ask yourself a question. Why would the Arabic language have over forty words for slave?

Abd means black slave and an African. Think about that for a moment. Abd means both black slave and African. There is an entire history in those two meanings.

There's a word for white slave—mamluk. There's a word for a Hindu slave. Perhaps you're beginning to gain some idea that over a long period of time Arabs have had a lot to do with the slave trade because you don't change a language overnight. It takes a long time to accumulate forty words for a slave.

Francis Bok was given a room with the animals in the barn[1]. They gave him some straw to lay on. This is interesting because when slavery is brought up to Muslims they will admit that it happened in the past but that it's long since passed and besides that they treated their slaves really well. Perhaps that message was not given to Francis Bok's masters because he slept in the barn with animals. He tried to escape but, was captured and beaten.

By the way, as soon as he escaped, the Arabic language had a new word for him. The Arabic language has a word for an escaped male slave. It has a word for an escaped female slave. And it has a word for an escaped child slave. The Arabic language has put a fine point on slavery.

Francis kept working and plotting and growing a little older and a little stronger. Finally he found an opportune time and he escaped and he set out on his own forced march. This time not a forced march to slavery but a forced march to freedom. He got to Egypt and managed to get to America where he works with an organization called Iabolish.com and they were the group that sponsored him to come to this university.

Francis was asked from the audience, "Who captured you?" And he said "Muslims". Then later someone said, "Muslims can react very violently, indeed they can kill you if they don't like what you say about them. Are you afraid for your own life in saying that Muslims captured and enslaved me?" His answer was memorable. He said, "I am now a free man. Now I can die because I will die as a free man." Think about that. I will die as a free man. You can learn more about Francis Bok by searching the Web under his name.

---

1   The author heard Mr. Bok give a lecture at a university in about 2004.

ISLAM AND THE SLAVE TRADE

Now let's stop and take a closer look at the white man's involvement with slavery. Did he show up on the coast of Africa in a wooden ship to get slaves? Yes he did. But he didn't go into the bush to get them. He went to the slave market where he bought them at a wholesale price in wholesale lots. Bills of sale, money and invoices were exchanged. He left with his boatload of slaves that he got from the Muslim slave trader. The Muslims had been trading slaves and capturing slaves in Africa since before Mohammed and the white man just represented a new market. That's all. Muslims had been enslaving before the white man and when white people put together the code that eliminated slavery and the slave trade, Muslims just kept on with their old business. They are not inhibited by the laws of the Kafir.

We know that Mohammed had black slaves. It says so in the Hadith. It says so in the Sira. So slavery is nothing new to Islam because slavery is the ideal in Islam. The ideal Muslim is the slave of Allah and indeed Mohammed called himself the slave of Allah, because there is no freedom in Islam. Everything has been prescribed. Everything you need to do has been recorded and laid out and your job as a Muslim is to be a slave to Allah and follow all the rules which includes the Sunna of Mohammed. A slave is the ideal Muslim. This is reflected in one of the Muslim names, Abdullah. Abd—slave; Allah—slave of Allah.

Islam has enslaved many peoples, including Europeans. It's estimated that a total of 25 million Africans have been sold as slaves and we know that about a million Europeans have been sold into slavery. Indeed, the one word that we have for slave comes from the Slavic people, the Slavs. The Muslims took many slaves out of Eastern Europe and the primary ethnic group they preyed upon were the Slavs. So we adopted the term "slave" from the poor Slavs.

There are different uses for different races of people as slaves. The Blacks were usually put into rough, hard work and frequently died at it. It was a death sentence to be a Black slave in the Saharan salt mines.

Whites were usually put to work in what we would call white collar jobs. They could even become leaders in the Army. The highest priced slave in the Meccan slave market for 1400 years never changed. It was always a white woman who brought the highest price. Writings from Medieval Islamic documents show that they were very free and open in discussing which race you used for which job. For instance the white woman was preferred as a slave of pleasure but if you could not afford her since she was the most expensive, then an Ethiopian woman, or as they called them then, Abyssinian woman, was the second best choice.

It is very unfortunate but this sale of white women was put in place by Mohammed. You see, Mohammed had all manner of slaves and his favorite sexual partner was a white woman. Her name was Miriam. She was a Coptic Christian. Well, since Mohammed's Sunna determines what everything shall be, this means that the preference of all Muslims who wish a slave of pleasure is the same that Mohammed had, a white slave. So the Sunna of Mohammed was very bad for white women.

There is an interesting special kind of slave that was used in Islam, that of the eunuch. Generally these were black male slaves and the castration process removed everything about the sex. Eunuchs are even referred to in the Koran because they can see the woman of the house unveiled. The Koran is very clear about slavery. It's quite desirable and it has only one limitation, you cannot enslave Muslims. Only Kafirs can be enslaved and poor Francis Bok, being a Christian, was a Kafir.

REALITIES OF ISLAMIC SLAVERY

Francis ran away to get his freedom but he might have escaped being a slave if he had chosen to become a slave of Allah, a Muslim. The rules of Islamic slavery is that it is good to free slaves because that brings a great merit with Allah, but you don't free a Kafir slave. So perhaps Francis could have converted to Islam and been freed through that path. But Francis Bok wanted to be a Christian. He did not want to be a Muslim so he had to take the only path open to him, which was flight.

The full history of slavery is not taught in any university in the United States. Nor is it easy to find books written that include the fact of Islam's role in world slavery. The only acceptable history of slavery is the 200 year white man It was the white man who actually did the most to stop the international slave trade. The British Navy was commanded to intercept all slave ships. This did not stop the Islamic enslavement of Africans.

Out of the 25 million slaves that were taken out of Africa, 11 million were sold in the Americas. The other 14 million were sold in West and North Africa where Islam is and in the rest of Asia.

There was a terrible side effect of slavery. For every slave captured, the slavers had to kill others. For instance, Francis Bok's parents were killed. The slavers showed up with armed troops, and kill all those who could defend their tribe. When the slavers finally killed all the defenders, they could then take the best of the survivors as slaves. The old, the sick and the very young were left behind, because they couldn't take the forced march that comes right after capture. The estimate of the collateral damage from taking one slave varies. Some of those who visited Africa during the peak slave trading days said that as many as ten had to die to produce one slave in the wholesale market. Others said no, only five. So using the lower figure we can see that out of the 25 million enslaved, there were over 100 million Africans, as much as 120 million Africans, who have died over the 1400 year period and that includes today. These figures never get talked about.

MOHAMMED AND HIS SLAVES

Now then, let's talk about Mohammed's role in slavery. He had slaves in his family. His first wife, Khadija, owned slaves. Indeed one of Mohammed's first converts was a Black slave and Mohammed himself owned Black slaves. Mohammed was deep into slavery. As a matter of fact, slavery was one of the chief ways he financed jihad. He was involved in having Kafir men killed so their women and children could be made slaves. He sent his own jihadists out on slave missions. He gave away slaves as gifts. He owned all kinds of slaves including males, females and Black slaves. He passed around slaves for the purpose of sexual pleasure of his companions—men who were his chief lieutenants. He stood by and prayed while others beat slaves. He shared the pleasure of forced sex with female slaves after conquest. He captured slaves and wholesaled them to raise money for jihad. One of his favorite sexual partners was a slave who bore him a son. He got slaves as gifts from other rulers. The very pulpit he preached from was made by a slave. Some of his cooks were slaves. He was treated medically by a slave. He had a slave tailor. He declared that any slave who ran away from his master would not have his prayers answered. Now that didn't work out for Francis Bok because he did escape from slavery. His prayers were answered because his prayers were to be free.

It is interesting to note how slavery falls into the line of Islam's two fundamental principles—submission and duality. Submission because who is more submissive than a slave? And duality because the Islamic doctrine creates a separate legal classification, an ethical classification for the slave.

It's no wonder that for all these years Islam has been involved in slavery because Allah likes a slave and Allah wants Muslims to enslave others, because after you keep them as a slave long enough, they will convert to Islam and if they don't, then their children will. The Koran and Islam see slavery as a great good.

Now you say to yourself, "If it's in the Koran, why don't they still do it?" In fact, Muslims are still involved in slavery. Women who are brought in from the Philippines to work in Saudi Arabia are treated as slaves, their passports taken away and they may never get back home. So Islam has always been involved in the slave trading business. It's there, it's in the Koran, it's in the Sunna and the only reason they don't do it openly anymore is they're simply not militarily strong enough. But slavery cannot be removed from the Islamic doctrine because unlike our constitution for instance, Islamic doctrine is eternal. It's permanent. It's forever.

AFRICA

When David Livingston was in Africa he saw the slave trade up close. He said that the paddlewheels on the boat he was on frequently hit slaves who had drowned in the river or the bodies of those who were killed in the process of trying to get slaves. He described a peculiar disease among slaves that the slave owners told him about. "The strangest disease I have seen in this country really seems to be broken heartedness and it attacks Kafirs who have been captured and made slaves. Speaking with many who later died from it, they ascribe that their only pain was to the heart and place the hand correctly on that spot. Some slavers expressed surprise to me that these men would die seeing that they had plenty to eat and no work. It really seems that they died of a broken heart."

He spoke with slave traders a long time about what they did and the Muslims told him that their object in capturing slaves is to get them into their possession and make them convert to Islam.

Now this history is quite sad, but the saddest thing about this whole history of Islam and slavery is that it's not taught. Our universities don't teach it. The universities don't even teach how white people were enslaved or how many Hindus were sold into slavery. It is not enough that slavery has been in our past. We must teach the complete history of slavery in our schools and universities. Only then can we fully understand this dreadful history.

Every Muslim is a slave of Allah. Slavery is Islam's dark secret. Islam has enslaved Europeans, Africans and Asians. Unfortunately, the Western intellectuals, including blacks, are determined to cover up Islam's crimes against humanity.

ETHICS

LESSON 9

Islamic ethics do not share anything with our ethics. Islamic ethics are dualistic. They have one set of rules for themselves and another set of rules for everyone else, the Kafirs. Kafirs can be deceived, robbed, murdered and raped. There is even a word for sacred deceit, *taqiyya*.

THE GOLDEN RULE

Ethics is the great divide between Islam and all other cultures, but before we look at Islamic ethics, let's look at our own. Our ethics are based upon the Golden Rule, treat others as you would be treated. Who are the others? The others are ALL others. There's no elimination of someone because of race, sex, ethnicity, religion. In our politics everyone is to be treated fairly and equally before the law and the Golden Rule leads to the concepts of what we call fair and what we call equal. Some may jump up and say, "But we don't do that all the time do we?" Here's what's important. No, it is true that we do not do that all the time because every person is pulled between two contradictory ideas. One is to treat others as they should be treated. The other idea is purely selfish and only look to ourselves. When we dwell on our own personal needs too much and start hurting or harming others, we can be corrected and brought back by remembering the Golden Rule.

So the Golden Rule lies behind our legal and ethical system.

DUALISM

Islam does not follow the Golden Rule. Indeed Islam explicitly denies the Golden Rule. The Koran never addresses humanity as a whole. Instead humanity is always divided into the Kafir and the believer, the Muslim. The Koran is very clear that the Kafir is to be treated differently from the believer and this treatment can be very violent. So this division into Kafir and believer eliminates the possibility of having a Golden Rule.

Islam therefore is dualistic. It has one set of rules for itself and another set of rules for the Kafir. There is no universal humanity.

The other difference between Islamic ethics and ours is that fundamentally there is not the concept of right and wrong in Islam. All ethics in Islam are based upon what Mohammed did and did not do, therefore the concepts are not right and wrong, but what is permitted and what is forbidden. Mohammed is viewed as the perfect ethical man. Every Muslim is to follow him and do what he did and say what he said. The ethics of Islam are determined by what Mohammed did and said, his Sunna. The rest of the ethics are found in the Koran.

DECEIT

Let us examine Islamic ethics through deceit. Let's read some ideas that have been given to us by Muslims. This is a quote from Ali Al Timimi, an internationally known Muslim scholar who had government clearance. He even worked with a former White House Chief of Staff, and was invited to speak to the military about Islam.

Publicly, Al Timimi denounced Islamic violence and said: "My position against terrorism and Muslim inspired violence against innocent people is well known by Muslims.[1]" But privately another picture emerged. Five days after the attacks on September 11th, he called them legitimate and rallied young Muslim men in his mosque to carry out more Holy war and violent jihad.

Another Islamic leader in this country, Abdurahman Alamoudi, who developed the Pentagon's Muslim chaplain corps and acted as a goodwill ambassador for our State Department, also denounced terror. "We are against all forms of terrorism" he claimed. Privately he raised major funds for Al-Qaeda and was caught on tape grumbling that Osama bin Laden had not killed enough Kafirs in the U.S. Embassy bombings[2].

In our culture we would call these men liars. But this does not apply to Islamic ethics because what these men were practicing was deceit. They were talking to Kafirs when they said those things. Let's see what Mohammed said about deceiving the Kafir.

In Medina there was a Jew named al-Ashraf. Al-Ashraf wrote a poem in which he condemned Mohammed and Mohammed at the mosque asked, "Who will rid me of Ashraf, the enemy of Allah and his prophet?" One of the Muslims said he would but a few days later Mohammed noticed that

---

1   *Infiltration: How Muslim Spies and Subversives Have Penetrated Washington*, by Paul Sperry, pg. 32.

2   "Government Links Activist to Al Qaeda Fundraising" Washington Post, July 16, 2005. http://www.washingtonpost.com/wp-dyn/content/article/2005/07/15/AR2005071501696.html

the task of killing al Ashraf had not been done so he went to the man and said "What are you doing?" The man said, "Mohammed, in order to kill Ashraf I will have to tell a lie". Then Mohammed said, "Say whatever you need to say."

The Muslim took a couple of his friends and went to al-Ashraf and said they were getting sick and tired of Mohammed, but before they could leave, they needed to have a little money and were wondering if al Ashraf could help. They wanted to borrow some money. Al Ashraf said he would need some collateral to loan you the money. And so they suggested that perhaps they could bring him their weapons—their swords and knives—and leave them in pawn. He agreed.

So the next night the three Muslims showed up, their weapons in hand. They had come to pawn the weapons. They chatted with him in a friendly way and said, "It is night, a pleasant night, let us go for a walk and discuss things". So they did. But in the middle of the walk after they had recited some poetry, one of them grabbed him by the hair of the head, said to the other, "kill him", and they knifed him in the stomach and killed al-Ashraf.

When they came back to Mohammed, Mohammed was delighted at the death of the enemy of Allah and the prophet[3]. He had given them permission to lie because they were dealing with a Kafir and the lie advanced Islam. Here we have dualism. A Muslim is told not to lie to another Muslim, but with a Kafir there is an option. The Muslim can tell the Kafir the truth or he can tell him a lie if it will advance Islam. And this was repeated many times in Mohammed's life. So much so at one point he said, "Jihad is deceit."

BESLAN

Now let's go back to the idea that Islam does not use terror. And let's take another story. This one happened in Russia in Beslan[4], where there was a school and the school had roughly a thousand people in it including the children and the personnel. Some Muslim jihadists attacked the school and took it over. The jihadists took all of the children and put them in the gymnasium. They were kept there for days without food or water. Finally the Russian special forces decided that they needed to go in. There

---

3   Bukhari 5,59,369. Also: *The Political Traditions of Mohammed*, CSPI, 2006, pg. 64.
4   "Carnage in Russian School Siege", CBS News, September 3, 2004 http://www. cbsnews.com/stories/2004/09/04/world/main641167.shtml

was chaos, and as the children jumped out the windows and ran for safety, the jihadists shot them in the back.

The attack continued. Once it became clear that they were going to lose the building the jihadists fell back on their original plan. They had brought explosives and placed them in such a way that when they detonated them, the roof fell in on the children. This was the way that most of the children were killed. This was a terrible attack, but what happened after the attack was this.

Muslim scholars and Muslim imams all said the same thing, "That was not Islam. In Islam we are forbidden to kill women and children." And that is true, there are hadith which state that women and children are not to be killed. However, there are other hadiths in which they're getting ready to attack a tribe and the reason they're attacking is these people are Kafirs, they had done nothing wrong. They decided to attack at night and they asked Mohammed what if they made a mistake in the dark and wound up killing women and children and Mohammed said, "They are from them."

Well now we have a contradiction. We have Mohammed saying—do not kill women and children and we have Mohammed saying kill them, they are from them. This is dualism. We have contradictory facts, but both of them are true. The jihadists can choose whichever they want and what did the jihadists in Beslan do. They chose to kill the children. Why? They are from them. That is, they are Kafirs.

THE ETHICS OF JIHAD

In Mohammed's time, in which he developed the ethics of jihad, he always had the Kafirs confused. The Arabs, just like everyone else, had rules for warfare. Since Mohammed was an Arab they kept expecting him to follow the rules, but Mohammed did not follow the rules. He made them up as he went alone.

So far as terror not being Islamic, Mohammed said in one of the most famous Hadiths, "I have been given five things that have never been given to anyone before me." One of these things that he was given was that Allah allowed him to spread Islam by awe and terror.

Jihad is terror. So when Muslim scholars say terror is not the way of Islam, they are practicing deceit. Indeed the practice of deceit even has a special name in Arabic, *taqiyya.*. It means sacred deception. To even have the concept of sacred deceit is an amazing ethical thought.

Here's another example of deceit in jihad. In modern times we have grown used to the fact that a Muslim jihadist can strap on dynamite and walk into a room filled with people and kill himself and everyone else.

Muslim clerics say that is not Islam because suicide is forbidden in Islam. And this is true. Suicide is forbidden in Islam. But there is a very famous Hadith in which Mohammed said that killing yourself while trying to kill Kafirs sends you straight to heaven, therefore the ethical expectation of the person who kills himself in the face of killing others is that he will go straight to heaven. He is a martyr.

In the very term martyr in Islam, we see the difference between the West and Islam, because the word martyr in Islam means someone who dies while killing Kafirs, whereas in our language the martyr is the one who is killed because of what he believes.

Here's another example of the ethical divide. Currently in America there is debate over whether waterboarding is torture. Indeed what constitutes torture is being talked about in the media. There is no debate inside the Islamic world about torturing Kafirs, and the reason is Mohammed tortured Kafirs. We know this because there's a famous story about when he attacked a tribe of Jews. After the Jews had surrendered, they took the leader of the Jews and staked him out on the ground at Mohammed's orders. The reason they did this was they knew that the Jews had a buried treasure. Mohammed had a small fire built on the old man's chest but he would not speak. He would not give up the secret of the treasure so finally Mohammed said cut him loose and he took him over to a jihadist who had lost a brother in the attack on the Jews. And he gave the brother the pleasure of killing the leader of the Jews. So as a consequence, there are no debates in Islam about whether torture can be used against Kafirs. It is Sunna. It is the way of Mohammed to torture the Kafir.

THE WHOLE TRUTH

Islamic ethics are clearly laid out in the Hadith. Here are some statements about Islamic ethics found in various traditions. A Muslim is to never cheat another Muslim in business. A Muslim does not lie to another Muslim. A Muslim does not kill another Muslim. A Muslim does not bother another Muslim's wife. These statements are very dualistic because this behavior is only reserved for other Muslims. A Muslim is a brother to other Muslims. Anyone who knows Muslims says "Wait a minute, I know a lot of Muslims and they don't lie to me and they don't cheat me in business. They don't come to work with dynamite and kill themselves and other people." This is duality. The Kafir has two ways of being treated. He can be treated just as a human being. The Golden Rule can even be applied to him if it will advance Islam, but the truth does not need to be told. The truth can be shaded. The most common form of this deceit is for Muslims to only discuss the Koran of Mecca. Only talking about the Koran of Mecca is telling a half-truth, not telling the whole truth.

In our courts, we swear to tell the whole truth and nothing but the truth. Nothing but the truth prohibits direct lies. But it's equally important to tell the whole truth because telling half a truth is just another form of a lie. So when a Muslim only discusses the Koran of Mecca, the "good" Koran, this is a form of deceit. All Muslims obey an ethical code which is quite different from our ethical code.

Islamic ethics support how Muslims treat women. For instance, women can be beaten. Women are set apart in their own separate code. There is an ethical system for slavery. Mohammed was the perfect slave master. His Sunna laid out all the ways that slaves are to be treated. There is an ethical system for the treatment of the dhimmi, that strange political creature who is not quite a slave, but certainly not a citizen.

So Islamic ethics lie behind everything that a Muslim does, but it does bring up political questions. If a Muslim does not have to tell the Kafir the truth, why would we use Muslim translators for Arabic documents at of the FBI and the CIA? Muslim translators take an oath, but Islam has a very unique interpretation of oaths, that is, an oath can always be changed by a Muslim for something better, and there is a Hadith which explicitly states this. But the Hadith does not really say what is better. That is the choice of the Muslim. So if we have a Muslim policeman or a military man who takes an oath to serve and protect, he can change it anytime he wishes. And for that matter, this same changing of oaths is applied to political treaties. If the Muslim nation signs a treaty with a Kafir, it can be abrogated at any time as long as Islam comes out on top.

To deal with Islam, it is critical that we understand its ethics. We assume that they're the same as ours but this assumption is based upon ignorance because Islamic ethics are very different from ours. Ours are based on the unitary law of treating all people the same. Islamic ethics are based upon the idea of Kafirs and believers and having a separate set of ethics for each one. One cannot understand Islam without understanding this ethical duality.

KORAN

The Koran must surely be the world's most famous book that has not been read. How many people do you know who can say "I have read the Koran and understood it"? It turns out that there are two Korans. Once you understand how they differ, you will understand Islamic duality and why Islam always has two stories about any subject.

The word Koran is an Arabic one and it means recitation. According to Islam, the Koran is perfect, complete, universal and final. It contains not the slightest error since it comes directly from Allah, the only God of the universe. It is in his exact words. The Koran was created before the universe was created and it sits on an emerald table at the right hand of Allah.

THE BOOKSTORE KORAN

The Koran we have today was created or brought together by the third caliph Uthman. It is said that Muslims were beginning to say that there were many versions of the Koran and there would soon be error. So Uthman, as absolute ruler, called in all of the Korans and turned them over to a secretary. It was the secretary's job to compile the new Koran. After it was put together Uthman did something that was very telling. He burned all the original source material.

Now ask yourself a question. Why did he burn the original source material if the reason that they had put together a new Koran was that there were variations?

As a result of the burning of all the source Korans, Muslims like to boast today that their Koran has no variations, that it was delivered in this exact form from Allah and the lack of variations shows it perfection. And then they point to variations in Biblical texts as proof of corruption of the texts.

Since Islam means submission, this argument that the Koran is perfect and the New Testament and Old Testament are corrupt and contain variations is another assertion that demands submission from the Christian and the Jew.

WHY IT IS HARD TO UNDERSTAND

The Koran contains 114 suras or chapters. If you pick up a Koran and thumb through it, you will notice very quickly that the long chapters are in the beginning and the short chapters are all at the end. That is the way that the Koran is arranged and this leads to one of the major difficulties in understanding it. Imagine if you took a mystery novel and cut off the spine and then you rearranged the chapters—you put the longest chapter up front and the shortest chapter at the back, then you took and rebound this book and handed it to a friend and told him, "This is a great mystery novel, read this." Your friend would try to read it and say, "I can't understand this, when I turn the page I seem to go back in time or sometimes forward in time. I don't understand, there's no story to this. There's no plot." And that is the way the Koran is arranged. Now if you take the Koran and put it in the right time order, then it is a much more logical book.

Another thing about the Koran that's confusing is that the stories in many cases are not complete. Every story has a beginning, a middle and an end, but most of the stories in the Koran many times are like you walked in halfway through the story. You don't know what the beginning is. This is odd since the Koran has obviously derived many of its stories from the Hebrew Bible, the Old Testament and they are wonderfully told, but not so with the Koran. There is not one really complete story in all of the Koran. There's always something missing.

A feature that stands out is how repetitious it is. This becomes very tiring when you're trying to read it. As an example, the story of Moses and the Pharaoh is repeated in some fashion 39 times. The repetition is so intense in the Koran that if you remove all of the repetition, it is cut in half and that does not leave a very big book, since the Koran is about the same size as the New Testament.

Something is a little odd about the stories. They fall into two classifications. There is some retelling of old Arabic stories and then there are the retelling of the Jewish stories—Adam, Noah, Moses, all of these characters appear in the Koran, but if you're familiar with the stories in the Jewish Bible, the Torah, they're not the same. They merely have the same characters. For instance, in the Koran it is the purpose of Moses not to free the Jews as slaves, instead to get the Pharaoh to admit that Moses is the prophet of Allah. The same is true with the story of Noah. The whole story of Noah centers around making the people of the earth admit that Noah is the prophet of Allah and because they would not admit that Noah was the prophet of Allah and do everything that he said, Allah destroyed the earth. So the stories are similar to the stories in the Old Testament, but they've all been changed so that they proclaim one theme—those who do not recognize the prophets of Allah will be destroyed.

It becomes apparent when you read the Koran is that much of it is devoted to the Kafir. As a matter of fact, 64% of the Koran is devoted to the Kafir[1]. That only leaves less than 36% to be devoted to being a Muslims. And that 36% is filled with repetition. So, the Koran is not a very big book at all when you get down to what does it mean to be a Muslim. There is not enough information in it to practice the religion of Islam. For a work which claims to be complete, it is remarkably incomplete. How to be a Muslim comes from the Hadith, the Traditions of Mohammed. Mohammed is the one who tells a Muslim how to worship, not Allah.

CONTRADICTION AND DUALISM

The other thing that strikes people who press on through and read the Koran is that it is very contradictory. One verse will contradict another verse. The Koran says Allah can replace a verse with one which is better. Let's dwell on this a moment. Replace it with a verse which is better means that the better one comes later. To deal with contradiction, you need to know which verse was written earlier or later. This time order is known to scholars. Although the Koran you buy in the bookstore is arranged from longest chapter to shortest chapter, Muslims have known which the right chronological order.

This cancellation of one verse by another later verse is called abrogation. But abrogation does not cancel or negate the verse because if the earlier verse was by Allah then that verse is true because, Allah by definition, cannot tell a lie. The Koran is contradictory, but both sides of the contradiction are true.

This turns out to be an insight into the mind of Islam because it means that Muslims can hold in their mind two contradictory ideas and accept both of them as true. This explains how Muslims after September 11th were able to say Islam is a peaceful religion. A peaceful religion doesn't send out jihadists to kill 3,000 people. That is a contradiction. But if you are a Muslim you have been trained to accept contradictory facts and so as a result these contradictions do not bother you at all, they don't cause you any mental problem. The Koran is a dualistic document. This dualism runs very deep into the Koran. If you arrange it in the right time order, the Koran written in Mecca is a radically different Koran than the one written in Medina. They are so different that you could take a class of college

---

1 http://cspipublishing.com/statistical/TrilogyStats/AmtTxtDevotedKafir.html

students and in one hour's time teach them how to pick out a verse taken at random and tell you whether it was written in Mecca or Medina. The two Korans are that different.

MECCA AND MEDINA

The earlier Koran is more religious. There are 147 different references to Hell. Over 90% of these say that the reason that the Kafir is burning in Hell is because he did not believe that Mohammed was the prophet of Allah. The remainder are people in Hell for morals charges—that is, theft, greed, hate. What does that tell us about Islamic Hell? It's a political prison for the intellectual dissenters who do not believe that Mohammed is the prophet of Allah and indeed the great majority of the Meccan Koran is devoted to that theme. Indeed the entire Meccan Koran can be summarized in one sentence: Mohammed is the prophet of Allah and if you don't believe it you're going to suffer.

Now the Koran written in Medina continues with the same hatred of the Kafir but it manifests in a totally different way. There's not much mention of Hell in Medina because a new form of suffering for the Kafir is introduced. In Mecca the Kafir suffers after he dies. In Medina he suffers in this life. He can be tortured, beheaded, robbed and worse. The Medinan Koran has the same Kafir hatred but this time there is jihad, where the Kafir suffers and dies in this life. So the Medinan Koran is very political.

The Medinan Koran introduces Mohammed's greatest innovation and that is jihad. It also introduces the dhimmi, the political subservience of the Christian and the Jew. Now as sure as someone brings up the violence in the Koran, someone is going to say "Oh, well the Koran is no different than the Old Testament, the Old Testament has a lot of violence in it as well." Yes, there is violence in the Old Testament but it's enormously different from the violence in the Koran. The violence in the Old Testament is local and temporary, it is against a neighboring tribe and for a certain period of time. This is not true of the violence in the Koran. The violence in the Koran is universal and eternal. The jihad is to go on until the last Kafir leaves the face of the earth. There's a great deal of difference between temporary, local violence and a universal, eternal violence.

Although jihad is called Holy War, it is really better described as simply political war. Why? Because the only reason in the Koran that people are attacked and killed is they do not agree that Mohammed is the prophet of Allah. That's an intellectual idea and so jihad is political war against the Kafir.

ARABIC

The Koran is an Arabic document. More than once it refers to its Arabic nature. That's very clear. Since the Koran was written before the creation and in the Arabic language, that implies that Allah is an Arab. This is a very important part of the Arabic hegemony, that is, the Arabic culture must dominate all other world cultures.

When you bring up something negative about the Koran, a Muslim quickly responds, "Oh, but did you read it in the Arabic?" And then he will say, "Well you can't really understand the Koran unless you read it in Arabic." Now let's stop and think about this statement for a moment. The Koran claims to be universal. That is, it applies to all people. But since only a small portion of the world reads Arabic that means these ideas must be understandable in languages other than Arabic or they would not be universal. So which is it? Can the ideas be understood in any other language or not, because if the ideas in the Koran cannot be understood in other languages, then the Koran is not universal.

The other weakness to the, "Oh, but you don't understand Arabic" is this. The great majority of Muslims today don't speak Arabic, so the Koran has been translated into their language and they're fully practicing Muslims.

Now, many Muslims recite the Koran in classical Arabic, but the classical Arabic is not the Arabic language of today. Languages change over time and a modern Arab cannot pick up a random Koran verse and read it and understand it. It's like if you study Chaucer. Chaucer wrote in the English of his day, but the English is very difficult for us to understand. It is the same with a native Arab speaker picking up the Koran and reading it. He, too, is not fully aware of what it means. He, too, has to have the classical Arabic translated into modern Arabic. The fact is that Arabic is no barrier to understanding the Koran. It's been translated into many languages.

In the end, the Koran is a document about the Kafir. 64% of it is about hating the Kafir and how the Kafir must be subdued, therefore the Koran is primarily a political document, not a religious document.

THE IDEAS OF THE KORAN

Now what does the Koran bring to the table that is new? It brings two new ideas. Mohammed is the prophet of Allah and jihad can be practiced against those who do not believe. Everything else in the Koran is derivative. There are old Arabic stories, stories from the Old Testament that have been reworked, ideas from the Zoroastrian religion, and ideas from the local Arabic religion at the time of Mohammed. It is interesting that the Koran claims to be the work of a universal God, but the horizon of the Koran goes no further than Mohammed's eyes.

THE SOLUTION

Until recently the Koran has been a document that is difficult to read. That is no longer true. *A Simple Koran* arranges all the verses in the right order and they've all been grouped so you eliminate most of the repetition, and Mohammed's life has been woven through the *Simple Koran*, so the reader can see that although the Koran claims to be a complete document, there are many, many things in the Koran that cannot be understood unless one knows the life of Mohammed. For instance, which verse comes earlier, which verse comes later? If you know Mohammed's life, it is easy to tell which one is earlier and which one is later. It is Mohammed's life that gives meaning to the Koran. The Koran cannot be understood on its own. And yet, it claims to be complete.

Here's a small example. In the Koran there is a remark about the destruction of the palm trees. The verse just comes out of nowhere. If you weave Mohammed's life into the Koran then you know what it means. Mohammed was given authority to burn the palm trees, because it was only a few days earlier that he had attacked the Jews. They had a date palm plantation which he burned, contrary to the rules of war. The Arabs condemned him for violating the rules of war. Hence, the Koran declares that it was good to burn the palm trees.

This is an example of how Mohammed's life gives meaning to the Koran and indeed when Mohammed's life is woven into the Koran, the Koran becomes an epic story. It depicts Mohammed's rise to power from being an orphan and a businessman to the supreme ruler of all of Arabia with a goal of becoming the supreme ruler of all of the world. So the Koran is a great epic story. You should read it and understand it.

The Koran has been made to seem complicated. It is actually a simple text that contains only two new ideas—Mohammed is the final prophet and jihad may be used to harm Kafirs. The main idea in the Koran is the division of humanity into believer and Kafir and the triumph of Islam over all Kafirs.

Note: *An Abridged Koran* is identical to *A Simple Koran* except all of the repetition has been removed. *A Two Hour Koran* is further condensed to 79 pages.

SUBMISSION AND DUALITY

Islam is based upon two principles—submission and duality. When you understand how these principles work you'll understand the political doctrine of Islam.

Islam's first principle is submission and that is declared in the very name Islam and Muslim. Islam means to submit and Muslim is one who has submitted.

Islam is a chain of submission. The ranking of authority is Allah, Mohammed, the Muslim, the Kafir, the dhimmi and the slave. In this country we are beginning to see how submission works. We're not as far along as Europe, but Muslims have immigrated here and have started making their demands. The first thing they have demanded is that the textbooks of America must conform to their way of teaching about Islam. No Kafir is allowed to write in the textbooks of America something that is critical of Islam. It all has to be vetted by Islam. Our textbook system has already submitted.

DUALISM

But submission is not enough to explain the success of Islam. Its most powerful principle is duality. Duality is the second major principle of Islam. We see duality in how the Koran and Mohammed's life are divided. First comes Mecca, where Mohammed is a religious preacher, who says that you have your religion, I have mine. Then comes Medina and jihad. You must submit in this life or Islam has the option of harming you. The two positions contradict each other, but both of them are equally true.

This duality explains Islam's overwhelming success. Islam has two phases that it manifests to the world. The face of Mecca and the face of Medina. Medina is the violent phase, the political phase. Mecca is the nice phase. What we have is that the Koran of Mecca is used as a shield. It's the Teflon coating. It's the public face of Islam. Mecca is what Muslims always talk about when they talk about Islam to Kafirs. This duality, this subtlety is what makes Islam so powerful because you can't just jump up and condemn Islam as being totally violent. Most Muslims are not violent at all, so therefore this charge doesn't work.

Duality is when Muslims say that anything that is based upon the Koran of Medina is not the real Islam—Osama bin Laden, 9/11, al Qaeda—oh that's not the real Islam. But the duality of Islam is that two contradictory things are both true. The Muslim friend, the nice Muslim at work, they're part of Islam. The real Islam actually includes the Muslim friend and Osama bin Laden. The real Islam includes the Koran of Mecca (religious) and the Koran of Medina (political).

When something dreadful happens such as the 9/11 destruction of the World Trade Towers, the London bombings, the Mohammed cartoon riots, Muslims say, "Oh, that is not the real Islam". It is, but they do not protest, they merely deny. Why don't they protest against the Medinan Muslims, the jihadists? Because they are outranked. The Medinan Koran that celebrates war and political power is higher and more powerful than the Meccan Koran.

THE WHOLE PICTURE

We need to see the entire truth of Islam. The whole truth, not the half-truth. That is the reason that understanding the principle of duality is an absolute necessity. If you do not understand the principle of duality you will always be fooled by the Koran of Mecca.

Let's see how duality can work in real life. There is a retired military man who is a devout Christian. He had some Muslim friends. They pointed out to him the verses in the Koran of Mecca that sounded very good to him and they said, "This is Islam." He says, "This is very good. This is like Christianity. I like this. And besides, the Muslims are such moral people, they don't drink, their women are very modest, they don't gamble. This must be the real truth of Islam." And off he goes into the market place of ideas proclaiming that Christianity and Islam are perfectly compatible. Indeed they're like brothers. Because of duality he does not understand that there is another truth, the truth of Medina. But his logic is a Western logic and it works like this. The jihad is contrary to the peace of Islam, so the jihad must be false because I believe in the truth of the peace of Mecca. Dualism has fooled him.

But dualism is used in all the words of Islam. They use the same words we do but they have entirely different meanings. Let's take for an example the word peace. Salaam. Now that sounds very nice, but when you understand what Islam means by peace it's not nice at all.

Peace in Islam comes only after you have submitted to Islam. The submission can be brought about by jihad. So here we have again the Koran of Mecca covers the Koran of Medina. That is, our common understanding of the word peace hides the fact that jihad can be used to achieve Islamic peace.

Here's another example of dualism—women's rights. Muslims are very quick to use the phrase women's rights and say that, Islam grants women rights. And this is true, but they are the rights to be beaten, the rights to inherit half as much, and the rights to have their testimony be worth half that of a man in court. This dualism allows a Muslim to look straight at a problem and not see the other half. After 9/11 Muslims protested, "Oh we are the religion of peace." They were able to maintain that because they're so used to having a dualistic view. They can accept the religion of peace as being absolutely true, whereas they know that jihad is one of the teachings of Islam. Dualism allows a Muslim to have a totally compartmentalized mind in which the Koran of Medina never interferes with the Koran of Mecca. But deep within the political doctrine of Islam we have duality and the Kafir.

Jihad demands complete submission from the Kafir and creates the Kafir as a completely separate social and political class. Islam allows its women to be beaten. Submission—Duality. Islam has separate set of rules for women and Kafirs.

HOW IT WORKS

Let's take a look at how the principles of submission and duality work with so many Islamic concepts. We've already discussed Islamic slavery and its fundamental principles. Submission and duality explain the whole process of slavery. Who submits more than a slave? Who is so separate and apart from us? Slaves fall under a separate moral code. So submission and duality completely explain the ethics of slavery.

We have the duality of a social and political class in the dhimmi who exists within an Islamic political system in which he is subjugated and not given full legal rights.

And of course the grand duality of all Islam—Mecca and Medina. Mecca must submit to Medina and the duality here is that you have two separate Korans that contradict each other, but both of them are completely true. We see submission and duality in Islam's ethics where we have one set of rules for the believer and another set for the Kafir. Islamic politics are dualistic. Mohammed, of course, is the chief dualist. His life divided into being the preacher, and then the successful jihadist-politician. Now Islam says it worships one, and only one god, but that god, Allah, is the God of duality and the God of submission whom everyone is to fear. The Koran says over 300 times that we are to fear Allah.

THE GOLDEN RULE AND ISLAM

Once you understand duality and submission, you really no longer have any need of the doctrine because everything that happens in Islam can be explained by those two principles.

Every political system has fundamental principles that underlie it. Our political system of democracy has the Golden Rule as a foundation. The Golden Rule underlies our goals of government. It is our moral and political guide. Treat others as you wish to be treated. We use the Golden Rule to criticize our own behavior. When we can clearly point out that something is unfair and abuses others, then the Golden Rule is the principle we use to fix that. It is our guiding principle, even if it is not something that we can always fulfill.

Islam denies the truth of the Golden Rule because the Golden Rule is the same for every person and Islam has two sets of behavior—one for the Kafir and the other for the believer.

We need to understand that there cannot be a compromise between submission and duality, and the Golden Rule. We would like to think that everyone can coexist peacefully, but Islam does not work like that. Islam demands submission. There is simply no compromise between a system that wants to use the Golden Rule and be democratic and another system which says that everyone has to submit. When they say everyone has to submit, Islam means everyone. Let's take some political examples.

What we now call Afghanistan used to be a Buddhist nation. It was a nation of peace and wealth. Then Islam invaded. Today in Afghanistan there is not a single Buddhist to be found. Not one. The only place you can find any Buddhism in Afghanistan is if you dig into the dirt like an archaeologist.

Islam keeps working until 100% of a civilization gives way to Islam. Today in Turkey it's 99.7% Islamic. Islam is working very hard to make sure that the other 0.3 of 1% disappears. Over a period of time every single Christian in Turkey will be gone. They will have immigrated or been killed in a street riot. Islam does not cease until submission is 100%. The entire time that it's making the Kafir submit,; it keeps proclaiming the truth of Mecca.

The principles of submission and duality contradict and deny the Golden Rule. We're going to have to study the laws of duality and submission.

Once you understand duality you will understand that Islam is grinding away very slowly at our own democratic rights.

THE THOUSAND YEAR PLAN

Islam has an overwhelming advantage over the Kafir. Islam has thousand year plan. Duality and submission are part of thousand year plan. Islam's duality and submission are like gravity. It never sleeps. It's always there. Always pressuring, always pushing. Submission must occur with the Kafir. If not now, tomorrow. Islam is very patient. Mohammed said in war patience is a virtue. Muslims study Mohammed and know that submission may take time, but Islam is very patient.

In Turkey it's taken them 400 years to get to the 99.7% mark of Turks being Muslim. They're not in a hurry. They can keep fooling the Europeans and say we're very democratic, but there you have another use of the word by Islam that does not mean what we mean. True democracy is not what Islam practices. True democracy would mean that the Kafir has an equal say with the believer. The Koran of Medina says that cannot happen. The Kafir must submit to the Koran of Medina. So democracy in Turkey is a sham and a fraud. It is a tool used to make the Kafir submit. Turkey's public face to the political councils of Europe is the Koran of Mecca. Turkey stands up and says we are a modern state—the veil or Teflon coating, the Koran of Mecca. Meanwhile the sword of the Koran of Medina is working. More Christians immigrate from Turkey all the time, just like they do in Iraq. In Iraq they form 3% of the population and 30% of the immigrants because they're unable to deal with submission in Iraq.

But in our country which is still yet free of duality and submission, we keep believing the Koran of Mecca. We are historically ignorant of the Koran of Medina and the principle of duality. The sweet words of the Koran of Mecca pour out of our media and our universities and our politicians' mouth and we think we don't have to worry, a peaceful Islam is here, a reformed Islam is here, we can relax, we can go back to sleep.

TEARS OF JIHAD

The Tears of Jihad refers to the deaths of 270 million people over a 1400 year period. They were all killed for the same reason. They did not believe that Mohammed was the prophet of Allah.

IT STARTS

After Mohammed died, Abu Bakr was elected caliph, Supreme Ruler of all Islam. He was to provide both spiritual guidance and political guidance. So he was a combination of pope and king. Abu Bakr spent his three years in office making sure that Muslim Arabs did not leave Islam. An apostate is one who wants to leave his religion and it is a capital offense in Islam. The apostasy wars continued during his entire time in office.

Umar was the second caliph after Abu Bakr died. He picked up where Mohammed left off because Mohammed's last efforts were all directed towards attacking the Christians north of Arabia. They were Kafirs. They had not submitted to Islam.

At this time, the Middle East was not remotely what we think of now. It was basically a Greek culture. The Greeks were sailors and businessmen and the Greek culture spread all around the rim of the Mediterranean, including Syria and Northern Egypt. North Africa was a Greek culture. And, of course, all of Anatolia (Turkey) was Greek. It was a highly sophisticated culture but it had overwhelming problems: age, degeneracy and decay.

The Greeks had been at war with the Persians for a long time. This continual war left both the Persians and the Greeks weak, so the 900 year rule of Greek culture in the Mediterranean was coming to an end. The Greeks were also very divided along religious lines. Christianity had several variations and the Greeks in Constantinople had a different kind of Christianity than was practiced in Jerusalem, Syria and Egypt. These divisions were strong enough to cause ill will. So this was the world that Umar invaded and conquered.

The conquest went so fast that Umar was not really left able to govern what he had, but he now had enormous wealth because Syria, Persia, Iraq, Egypt and North Africa all fell in thirty years time. All of the Greek culture except that which was in Anatolia was destroyed. An entire new world order came about.

THE DHIMMI

At first the Christians were left pretty much to govern themselves and only send taxes to Medina. After the consolidation of the empire under Uthman (the third caliph), things began to change. Islam was no longer conquering more territory, instead it was consolidating. The age of the dhimmi had arrived. Being a dhimmi involved paying heavy taxes, but it also began to involve being a second class citizen in your own home country. In Egypt, for instance, the Coptic culture was especially despised. Now the Copts, the descendants of the Pharaohs, were Christian. Islam invaded a Christian and Coptic Egypt. Today Egypt is Arabic and 90% Muslim. Centuries of being a dhimmi annihilated Coptic culture. That was the life of the dhimmi.

North Africa became Islamic. 600 years of Christianity disappeared. The culture of the Greeks, the Romans, the Europeans, was all annihilated. Then the pressure started up against Greek Anatolia.

Now then everywhere the Muslims looked, they saw Christians who were wealthy, educated and very sophisticated. The Arabs were none of these things. The 900 year old world of the Middle East completely changed. And notice something, it has not changed in the last 1400 years except to become even more Islamic.

The Christians had no idea what hit them. They never called the invaders Muslims, instead they called them Arabs or Saracens. A Christian bishop of Jerusalem in the year 637 wrote of the "villainous and God hating Saracens" who burned cities, destroyed crops, set churches on fire, and left a train of destruction.[1]

From the beginning, the Christian leaders showed an incomprehension about the jihadist invasion. They called the invaders all manner of cruel names, except Muslim jihadists. Church leadership blamed the invasion on evil, but not Islam. From the very beginning, Christians were unable to look Islam in the eye and call it for what it is. Little has changed in Christian leadership in 1400 years.

Christianity has always been marked by divisions. When the members of one group of Christians saw another group destroyed by jihad, they reasoned that God was punishing those other "false Christians". Of course,

---

1 *The Legacy of Jihad*, Andrew Bostom, Prometheus Books, 2005, pg. 386.

only a little time later, they became the victims, as well. Again, there was no comprehension of the true nature of Islam.

After conquest, Islam controlled the Christian leaders by force. Orthodox patriarchs such as Alexander II and Christopher of Antioch were murdered for the good of Islam.[1]

Local Arabs helped the Muslims to invaded what is now Iraq, a Christian nation. Muslims destroyed monasteries, killed monks, burned churches, and forcefully converted Christians. All of this took place in the years 635 and 642.[2]

Islam invaded Palestine, Syria, Mesopotamia, Persia and Armenia. The country side suffered raids. Those who escaped were enslaved, the women raped and a fifth of the booty sent to the caliph. Jihad paid its own way as it went.[3]

After conquest came the dhimmi status, a semi-slave. They could still have their church buildings, those that were left. Christianity could not be seen or spoken of beyond the church or the home. For a Christian to try to convert a Muslim was a death sentence.

Christians were actually forbidden to read the Koran. This element is important because it helps to ensure the ignorance of the Christian. This has had a 1,400 year effect. Christians or other Kafirs still do not study either the history or the doctrine of Islam. To not study the history or doctrine of Islam makes anyone including, a Christian, a dhimmi.

Dhimmitude starts with ignorance. The cure for dhimmitude is knowledge. Once a dhimmi becomes aware of the doctrine of persecution and the history of persecution, the dhimmi's eyes are opened and the dhimmi becomes a Kafir.

The destruction in Anatolia took several hundred years. We have one accounting from a Muslim historian who gladly reports the destruction of 30,000 church buildings.[4] Now some of the better church buildings had a special fate reserved for them. Those sites became mosques. When it conquers, Islam has built its mosques on top of where the best church building or temple was. It is ever thus because this is the way of Mohammed or Sunna.

---

1 Ibid, pg 394.
2 *The Decline of Eastern Christianity*, Bat Yeor, Associated University Press, 1996, pg. 46.
3 ibid, pg. 47.
4 *The Legacy of Jihad*, Andrew Bostom, Prometheus Books, 2005, pg. 392.

MOHAMMED AND RELIGIOUS DESTRUCTION

Destroying religious art is also the way of Mohammed. As soon as Islam conquered any town, the churches were desecrated. The Christians could move back into them later if Islam decided to let them stand. Art, in particular religious art, is an affront to Islam. Mohammed's first act on returning to Mecca, after he prayed, was to destroy all the religious art[5]. We see this along the silk route where all of the Buddhist murals in caves have had the eyes pecked out and the mouth taken out.

There was an interesting side effect for those who had already been conquered as the conquest ebbed and flowed in Constantinople. If the Arabs lost a battle in Constantinople, there would be riots of anger that the Christians had beat the Muslims and the Christian dhimmis would be killed.

This persecution was what set the stage for the Christians in the Middle East to cry out to their brothers in Europe. So the history of the crusades is one of the few times where Christians tried to help other Christians in the Middle East. The Crusades should be studied to see what can be done now to help Christians against Islam.

ASIA

In the East, jihad was not just against the Christians, it was against everyone. The Persian Empire at this time had already been crushed. Zoroastrianism, the religion of the Persians, was annihilated. It was annihilated to such a degree today that historians are not really sure of the true nature of the Zoroastrian religion because so many of their sacred texts were destroyed.

Islam moved towards Hindustan. Due to jihad, what we think of as India today is about half of its original territory. But on the way to Hindustan, Islam stopped off in Afghanistan and destroyed the Buddhism that was there.

They then turned to the Hindus. The attack against the Hindus was similar to the ones against the Christians, Buddhists and Persians. When Islam started attacking the Persians, there was a parlay, a conference before the battle and the Persian general asked "Who are you and why are you here?" because the Persians had never really fought the Arabs. And here, in a hadith, is what Islam told him. "Our prophet, the messenger of our Lord has ordered us to fight you until you worship Allah alone or pay

---

5 *The Life of Muhammad,* A. Guillaume, Oxford University Press, 1982, pg. 552.

the jizya, the dhimmi tax, and our prophet has informed us that our Lord says whoever amongst us is killed shall go to paradise and lead a life of great luxury. Whoever amongst us remain alive will become your master."[1] This is the perfect statement of jihad.

The reason for invading Hindustan was exactly the same reason as invading Persia and it was the same reason for invading Anatolia (Turkey) and the Middle East. It's important to realize this because many times people think that when the Muslims invaded maybe the people there got what was coming to them in some way. No, their only fault was to be Kafirs.

THE ANNIHILATION OF THE HINDU

Just as the culture of the Middle East was crushed, the culture of the Hindu was crushed. You need to know that the Hindu that we see of today is not the Hindu before Islam. Islam changed the Hindu. Before Islam the Hindus had been a proud culture. They were a leader in intellectual theory, mathematics and philosophy. And they were very wealthy.

Hindustan had been an Empire for a thousand years and it had been relatively peaceful. In times of peace you accumulate great treasure. That was one of the things that happened in Afghanistan with the Buddhists. They were very prosperous because they had given up war. It turns out that the Buddhists teach us what happens when you deal with Islam on the basis of peace. What happened to the peaceful Buddhist was that the pacifists were annihilated. Witness the fact that half of the Hindu culture still remains behind because it had a warrior caste. None of the pacifist Buddhist culture remains in Afghanistan.

There were three waves of jihadic invasion into what we now call India. The first battle in 712 AD was at Debal, near Karachi. All males over the age of 17 were murdered and the women and children put into slavery.[2]

The second wave came in 1000 AD into northern India. The third wave came in 1206 AD. The brutality was massive. Death, rape, enslavement and civilizational annihilation were the results.

In the end the Hindus were crushed. Half their territory was gone. They were sold into slavery. There are some remnants of this in the geography books. In Afghanistan there is a mountain range called the Hindu Kush. Hindu Kush means the funeral pyre of the Hindu.

---

1   *Sahih Bukhari* 4, 53, 386
2   *Islamic Jihad*, M. A. Khan, iUniverse, 2009, pg. 194.

GHANDI, THE PIOUS TRAITOR

What we now call Pakistan was an original part of India. The British partitioned Pakistan from India so that it would become purely Islamic. It led to the destruction of about a million Hindus in the partition that led to the creation of the state of Pakistan.

It was Ghandi, the secular saint, whose pacifism and dhimmitude lead to the deaths of the million Hindus. It was Ghandi, who said that although all of the Hindus had to leave Pakistan, none of the Muslims in India had to leave. Today, Muslims are devouring India from the inside. Ghandi was the great betrayer of Hindu culture.

Both Ghandi and the Buddhists of Afghanistan show how pacifism leads to total annihilation in the shortest time.

At the other end of India in Bangladesh the Islamization goes on still today. In 1947 Bangladesh was still about one third Hindu. Today it is about 9% Hindu.[3] And that reduction has come at a terrible cost. Women and men who are left in Bangladesh are persecuted on a daily basis, dreadfully, and the police turn a blind eye when some Muslim throws acid in a Hindu woman's face. Why does he throw the acid? Her face isn't veiled. The police will not investigate because the police are Muslim.

We do not have time in this brief accounting to tell the terrible story of the conversion of Anatolia to Turkey. Nor do we have time to tell the terrible persecution of the Orthodox Christians in Eastern Europe.

JIHAD TODAY

The first September 11th was in 1683 when the Europeans drove the Muslims from the gates of Vienna. Of course some years later we would have another September 11th. Now what is important about that is this: Islam never forgot that on September 11th they had been turned back from the gates of Vienna and the proud Turkish Army defeated. They never forgot.

In America we had no idea why that date was chosen. We were clueless and in that ignorance we see the nature of Islam and the Kafir. The Kafir never remembers the history that went with the expansion of Islam. Islam never forgets. If we are not to submit, we must learn before we can remember. And we must educate others to open their eyes to the history of Political Islam.

---

3   [Bangladesh Bureau of Statistics] UK Border Agency, Bangladesh, August 11, 2009   http://www.ecoi.net/file_upload/1226_1252051940_bangladesh-190809.pdf

Since 9/11 there have been more than 16,956 jihad attacks.[1] All of this suffering goes on around the world and you never hear about it because our press does not want to report the terror of what is happening politically around the world with Islam.

But we can't blame our press because none of our schools, not even the Christian schools teach the dreadful history of the destruction of 60 million Christians. No schools teach the deaths of 10 million Buddhists, 80 million Hindus and 120 million Africans.

If we don't know the history we are doomed to repeat it. Islam continues to kill the Kafir and the Kafir just says, "Oh well, we'll take care of that problem by pretending it is not there. We absolutely refuse to admit that this is a culture that is devoted to the annihilation of our Kafir culture. When you go to Iraq, you don't find a Christian Iraq. When you go to Egypt, you don't find a Christian Egypt. They are both Islamic.

There's only one way to stop this. The history of the Tears of Jihad must be taught in Kafir schools. How can it be that the history of the expansion of the empire of Islam is treated as a glorious history and the history of suffering, the suffering of the dhimmi and the death of 270 million never reported? Until this changes we are doomed to continual annihilation both here in America and abroad.

---

1   www.thereligionofpeace.com. The date of the record is March 19, 2011.

CONCLUSION

Kafirs have a basic instinct when faced with Islam—let's make some compromises. We will do things your way, Islam can reform and life will be good.

We must go through all of the steps of compromise to see why it will not work. In particular, we must see why reform is a logical impossibility. And last, but not least, we must see why the "good" Muslim cannot and will not help to achieve a solution.

But since most Kafirs don't know anything about the history of Islam, they think that we will work this out like we always have. We will find a compromise. After all, in Kafir civilization, progress is made through teamwork and compromise. The first and crucial error is thinking that Islam is analogous to our civilization and that our rules apply to it. Let's compare the ideals of Islamic civilization with our civilization's ideals.

COMPARING IDEALS

Freedom Of Expression

First, the ideal Muslim has no freedom, but is a slave of Allah and the Sunna. There is no freedom of expression because that would mean that you could disagree with Islam. There can be small cultural choices, but there are very strong boundaries to Islam.

Mohammed laid the perfect example of freedom of expression when he finally gained power in Mecca. In the beginning when he had no power in Mecca, he allowed argument about his doctrine. After he was driven out of Mecca and later returned as its conqueror, he issued death warrants against all of those who had disagreed with him. When Mohammed died, there was not a single person left in Arabia who disagreed with him. Intellectual subservience to Mohammed/Islam was total. The Sharia denies freedom of expression. Islam tolerates discussion of Islam only when it is getting started and is politically weak.

Freedom Of Religion

If you are a Muslim and want to leave Islam, you become an apostate. An Islamic apostate can be killed. An apostate is worse than a Kafir. The Koran says that apostasy is a crime worse than mass murder.

But doesn't Islam preach that Christians, Jews and Muslims are all members of the Abrahamic faith? Is that not freedom of religion? But look more closely at what Islam says about Christians and Jews. Islam teaches that true Christians are those who say that Jesus was a Muslim prophet; there is no crucifixion, no resurrection and no Trinity. The only true Jews are those who admit that the Torah is wrong and that Mohammed was the last in the line of Jewish prophets. Otherwise, you are not a Christian or Jew in the eyes of Islam. So much for tolerance. In Islam the only real Christians and Jews are dhimmis, since they must declare their own scriptures to be corrupt and that Mohammed is the last prophet of both Jews and Christians. Those who don't are not true Christians and Jews by Islamic standards, but Kafirs.

And what about the atheists, Buddhists, Hindus, Jains, and on and on? They are all hated Kafirs just like Christians and Jews.

If there is freedom of religion, explain how every Muslim country becomes totally Islamic after enough time? Explain this in terms of freedom.

Slavery

The Koran sanctions and encourages slavery. Mohammed was the perfect slave owner, slave wholesaler, slave retailer, slave torturer and sex slave user.[1] Even though Islam sold Americans every slave[2], Islam has never acknowledged this fact nor apologized. None of this history can be found in a textbook.

Criticism

In our culture, we have the ability to criticize our own actions and the action of our political and religious leaders and correct mistakes. Criticism of Islamic religion or politics by Muslims is rare and can lead to a painful end.

---

1   *Mohammed and the Unbelievers*, Bill Warner, CSPI Publishing, 2006, pg. 154.

2

Freedom of the Press

Due to the publication of the Danish Mohammed cartoons, buildings were burned, people were killed, and almost no newspaper would reprint these political cartoons. You can say anything you want about Islam as long as Islam is not offended. Freedom of the press is forbidden in Sharia law.

Equal Justice Under the Law

The Koran specifically says that justice is served with different penalties for Muslims and Kafirs. A Muslim is not to be killed in retaliation for killing a Kafir. A Kafir may not testify against a Muslim in Islamic law. The entire Sharia law is based upon one set of laws for Muslims and another set of laws for Kafirs.

Ethics

Our ethics are based upon the Golden Rule, with all people considered equal. Islam is based upon dualistic ethics, with one set of rules for Muslims and another set of rules for Kafirs. Kafirs are hated by Allah and are targeted for annihilation by Mohammed. Kafirs must be subjugated. Islamic ethics are dualistic—Muslims are treated well and Kafirs are treated as second-class citizens or worse, if it is deemed necessary.

Women

In Islam, women are subjugated to the males. In court they are treated as half of a man and they are equal only on Judgment Day. Both the Sunna and the Koran say that wives can be beaten.

Torture

Torture is allowed in the Sunna and the Koran recommends cutting off hands and feet and crucifying Kafirs. Mohammed repeatedly tortured Kafirs, even to death. Torture of Kafirs is Sunna, the way of Mohammed.

Separation of Church and State

Our Constitution separates the church and state, but Islam demands that religion and state be combined as one unit. Sharia law includes both religious and secular law without distinction. Islam is a theocracy.

Friendship

Surely friendship is one of the most basic aspects of being human. But Mohammed was never the friend of a Kafir. His uncle, Abu Talib, adopted him, raised him, taught his business trade and protected him from harm by the Meccans. When he died a Kafir, Mohammed's first words were to condemn him to Hell. There are 12 verses in the Koran that say that a Muslim is not the friend of a Kafir.

Human Rights

There are no human rights in Islam, because there is no humanity in the Koran, just believers and Kafirs. Kafirs have no rights. Kafirs are hated by Allah and are lower than animals.

Since Islam does not have a point of agreement with our civilization, there is no way to find any compromise. Islam is not part of our civilization and does not play by our rules. How do you compromise with a civilization based on the principles of submission and duality?

REFORM?

The magical thinking of many intellectuals is that Islam can be reformed, like Christianity and Judaism experienced. This sounds great. Islam changes its ways and settles down to live among fellow humans.

Only this will not work because Islam was designed so it could not be reformed or changed. Why do we want to reform Islam? Do we care if Muslims pray three times a day instead of five times? No. The only reason we want reform is because of the violence against us. We do not want to reform the religion of Islam; we want to reform Political Islam.

THE PROBLEMS OF REFORM

The Koran is perfect, complete and universal. The Koran says that Mohammed is the perfect model of a Muslim. The first problem is the perfection of the Trilogy—a perfect Koran and a perfect Sunna. How do you reform perfection? Why would Muslims want to improve perfection? If you take something out of the Koran, was the item you removed imperfect? If so, then the Koran was not perfect. Do you see the problem with reforming perfection?

The other problem with reformation is the amount of detail in the Sunna. The Sira is 800 pages long and Mohammed is on every page. Then there are the 6800 hadiths in Bukhari. The Sunna is vast and covers the smallest detail, down to how many times to breathe when you drink a glass of water.

There is too much material for the doctrine to be reformed. For instance, 67% of Mohammed's prophetic career is about jihad[1]; it is not as if you can turn a blind eye to a few items and achieve reformation. Cutting out 67% of the Sira does not reform it, but creates a completely new text.

Islam will never eliminate the one concept that has brought it success, jihad. All of Islam's success has been based upon political submission, dualism and violence. Demanding the Kafirs' submission and using violence works for Islam. The violence is not going to stop because it has worked for 1400 years and is working better today than any time in the past.

THE GOOD MUSLIM

There is an attempt to make the problem of Islam go away by thinking that it is the "good Muslim" who will save the day. What is a good Muslim? What an apologist means by a good Muslim is one who is pleasant. But that point of view is not Islamic. Islam is the one and only basis of determining what a good Muslim is. An apologist's opinion of "good" is not relevant to anyone, except to the apologist and his friends. Islam says that a good Muslim is one who follows the Koran and the Sunna. That is the one and only criteria of being a good Muslim.

Apologists think that good Muslims are a proof of a "good" Islam and that the doctrine makes no difference. Oddly enough, Muslims do not agree with this. Muslims have one and only one definition of what a "good Muslim" is, one who has submitted to Islam and follows the Koran and the Sunna. The cause is Islam; the effect is Muslim. Apologists think that Islam submits to Muslims, but apologists are ignorant, free of facts, and in the soil of ignorance, any fantastic flower grows.

There are three kinds of Muslims. The first kind is the Meccan Muslim, a Muslim who is primarily a religious person without the jihadic politics. A Medinan Muslim is a political Muslim. Then there is the Muslim who follows the Kafir Golden Rule, instead of Islamic ethics.

A Golden Rule Muslim is one who is an apostate to some degree. Maybe the Golden Rule Muslim drinks beer or doesn't go to the mosque. All Muslims have some Kafir in them. The Kafir civilization has much to offer. Some Muslims prefer Kafir civilization to Islamic civilization in many ways. The assumption that every Muslim represents Islam in all that they do is wrong. There are many people who are good people who call themselves Muslim, but their goodness come from their humanity.

---

1   http://cspipublishing.com/statistical/TrilogyStats/Percentage_of_Trilogy_Text_Devoted_to_Jihad.html

EDUCATION

We have to ask this question. Why do our tax dollars fund universities that do not teach the doctrine of Political Islam? It is not taught at any university. How can this be? Why can't our tax dollars be used to teach the history of 270 million dead? Why can't our tax dollars be used to teach the real complete history of slavery?

By educating yourself, you are making a difference. By encouraging others to learn about Political Islam, you can make a huge difference. This war is not a war against terrorism. This war is a war against ignorance. And the enemy is not Islam. Islam is simply a doctrine. The enemy is our own passive ignorance. We must do battle against ignorance.

It is not that Islam is so strong. The problem is that our ignorance makes us weak.

FOR MORE INFORMATION AND MORE BOOKS

Go to: www.politicalislam.com

GLOSSARY

ablution, a ritual washing to become clean for religious acts.

abrogation, the Koran is filled with verses that contradict each other. The doctrine of abrogation is that the verse that is written later is better than the earlier verse.

Abu Bakr, Mohammed's closet Companion and his father-in-law, the first caliph.

Abu Talib, Mohammed's uncle, who adopted him, taught him how to be a caravan trader, and protected him in his role as a tribal elder. He died a Kafir and was condemned to Hell by Mohammed.

ahadith, the Arabic plural of hadith; hadiths is used in English.

Aisha, Mohammed's favorite wife of the harem. He married her when she was six and consummated the marriage when she was nine. She was eighteen when he died. Many of the hadiths are from her.

Ali, Mohammed's cousin and son-in-law. He is considered the head of the Shia sect and was the fourth caliph (the first caliph, according to the Shias).

Ansars, the Helpers. The Ansars were the first converts in Medina and gave money and shelter to the Muslims who left Mecca to go with Mohammed.

apostate, one who has left a religion, in particular, Islam. The Koran says that apostasy is the worst sin possible. It is far worse than mass murder. Mohammed and Abu Bakr killed apostates.

Black Stone, a dark stone, roughly seven inches in diameter. It is set into the corner of the Kabah in Mecca. It was there before Mohammed.

caliph, a political and religious leader of Islam, roughly a pope-king.

circumambulate, to move in a circle around the Kabah while praying.

companion, one who knew Mohammed. When spelled Companion it refers to most important companions: Abu Bakr, Umar, Uthman and Ali.

Copt, Copts were the original Egyptians, their ancestors included the pharaohs.

dhimmi, a Kafir who is "protected" by Islam. A dhimmi has no civil rights, for instance, cannot testify in courts against a Muslim. Today, a dhimmi is a Kafir who defers to Islam, an apologist for Islam.

Five Pillars of Islam, praying five times a day; paying the zakat, the Islamic tax; fasting during Ramadan, going on pilgrimage to Mecca; and declaring that there is no god, but Allah and Mohammed is his prophet.

Gabriel, an archangel of Allah, who relayed the Koran to Mohammed.

ghira, absolute control of a woman's sexuality in all of its forms is part of a man's ghira (pride, honor, self-respect and sacred jealousy).

hadith, a Tradition, or small story, about what Mohammed said and did.

Hadith, a collection of hadiths.

haj, (hajj), the pilgrimage to Mecca.

Helpers, the first Muslim converts of Medina who helped the Muslims who came from Mecca, known as the Ansar in Arabic.

Holy Spirit, the archangel, Gabriel, in Islam.

Hudaybiyya, an area near Mecca. It is famous because Mohammed was recognized as a political leader when he signed a treaty there. It is important to Kafirs because Mohammed showed that Islam only enters into treaties when weak and will break them when it becomes strong.

imam, an Islamic religious leader of the Sunni sect.

immigrants, those who left Mecca with Mohammed.

isnad, the chain of witnesses who relayed a hadith. The source person must have personally heard and saw what they reported. The hadith were recorded 200 years after Mohammed's death, so there is a long chain of who said what to whom.

jihad, struggle, also fighting in the path of Allah. It is much more than killing or war. All effort for the supremacy of Islam is included. Writing a letter to the editor about Islam, making demands on employers or voting for a Muslim candidate are all jihad.

jinn, a conscious being on earth, made of fire. Our genie is taken from this. They can work for good or bad. The Koran says that some of them are Muslims.

jizya, a special tax on Kafirs in Islamic countries. In history texts it is called a poll tax and can be as high as 50% of the income.

Kabah, a stone building, cubic in shape, measuring about 30 feet by 30 feet and 30 feet high. The Black Stone is mounted in a corner. There is no Islam without the Kabah.

Kafir, a nonbeliever, a non-Muslim. The lowest form of life, cursed by Allah

mullah, an Islamic religious leader of the Shia sect.

prostrations, lowering yourself to the ground while praying, part of Islamic prayer.

Quraysh, Mohammed's tribe.

rightly guided caliphs, the first four caliphs—Abu Bakr, Umar, Uthman and Ali. They were very close to Mohammed.

Saed, one of Mohammed's close Companions. He gave the judgment that lead to the beheading of 800 male Jews.

Safiya, a Jewess who married Mohammed after he killed her husband, cousin and tortured her father to death.

Sharia, Islamic law based upon the Koran, Sira and Hadith. In it all Kafirs are second class citizens, at best. Islam has the goal of replacing our Constitution with Sharia law.

Shia, those who follow Ali, about 10% of Muslims, strong in Iran and southern Iraq. The differences between the Shia and the Sunni are mainly political. They are willing to kill each other, but are united against the Kafirs.

spirit, the archangel Gabriel.

Sunni, those who follow the Sunna. They are about 90% of Muslims. The difference between Sunni and Shia is mainly political and is over who can be caliph.

Sunna, what Mohammed did and said is called the Sunna. It is the ideal pattern of Islamic life, the way of Mohammed.

sura, a chapter of the Koran.

Sira, the life of Mohammed by Ishaq, *Sirat Rasul Allah*. It is one of Islam's three sacred texts, the Trilogy.

Sufism, a mystical form of Islam. It was adopted from Hinduism and Buddhism by conquered Kafirs who converted to Islam.

Torah, the first five books of the Old Testament.

Trilogy, the three sacred texts of Islam—the Koran, the Sira (Mohammed's biography) and the Hadith (what Mohammed did and said).

Umar, the second caliph. He created the Islamic empire.

umma, the Muslim political, religious and cultural community. A Muslim is a member of the umma, before he is a citizen of any country.

Uthman, the third caliph, a close Companion of Mohammed. He was assassinated by Muslims.

zakat, a charity tax on Muslims, one of the Five Pillars. It is usually 2.5% of wealth.

CPSIA information can be obtained at www.ICGtesting.com
Printed in the USA
LVOW12s0004040515

437108LV00002B/4/P